Contents

1 At war in French Indo-China: 1941–54

Independence for the Vietnamese

▶ *How did the Second World War make a war of independence in Vietnam more likely once the war had ended?*

Origins of the conflict

The history of modern Vietnam starts in the 1870s and 1880s when French armed forces completed their conquest of French Indo-China and made it part of their empire (Source A). It was still in French hands at the start of the Second World War. At that time Vietnam was divided into three areas (see map on page 6). Tongking was in the north, Cochin China in the south, and Annam in between.

Source A The palace of the French governor in Saigon in the 1870s (top), and Vietnamese homes (below). Houses like these could still be seen in parts of French Indo-China in 1939.

The Second World War

At the start of the Second World War, French Indo-China was ruled in name only by an Emperor called Bao Dai. In reality, it was still a French colony. The cosy world of the colonialists was shattered for ever, however, when war broke out in 1939. Defeat in Europe made it impossible for France to protect her vast overseas empire. When the Japanese made a 'request' to move their troops to French Indo-China in July 1941, the French authorities were too weak to refuse. Five months later, Asia and the Pacific were at war. A remarkable rebel leader, Ho Chi Minh, came back to Vietnam at this time. He joined with other Nationalists and Communists to fight against the foreign invaders.

Ho Chi Minh (1890–1969)

Ho Chi Minh was born in central Vietnam. His name then was Nguyen Sinh Cung. He later took the names of Nguyen Tat Thanh, Nguyen Ai Quoc (Nguyen the Patriot) and eventually Ho Chi Minh (Ho the Enlightener). He spent most of his younger days in Europe – first as a chef in a London hotel and later as a political activist in France and the Soviet Union. He was trained as a revolutionary in Moscow at the Stalin School for the Toilers of the East. Ho returned to French Indo-China in 1940 to lead the independence movement against the Japanese. Ho was much admired – even by Americans (Source **B**).

Source B By the American journalist, C. L. Sulzberger

There is no doubt that soft-voiced little Ho Chi Minh, a man of simple personal habits, undoubted bravery and vast stubbornness, has captured the mind of a vast number of South-east Asian peoples still struggling to shrug off the last vestiges [traces] of nineteenth-century colonial subjugation [control]. There is also no doubt that Ho Chi Minh is a Communist.

From *A Long Row of Candles* by C. L. Sulzberger, Macdonald, 1969

The Vietminh

In 1941 Ho Chi Minh founded a resistance movement: the 'Viet Nam Doc Lap Dong Minh Hoi' ('League for the Independence of Vietnam'). In its early days, the Vietminh (as it was known) accepted members of many different political opinions. All were united by the desire to fight for freedom for Vietnam from both the Japanese and the French.

In the last years of the Second World War (1943–45), the Vietminh fought a very successful guerrilla campaign against the French and Japanese. They were led by a brilliant military leader and former history teacher, General Vo Nguyen Giap. He trained an élite group of men and women guerrillas to fight in the jungles of Vietnam (Source **C**). Dressed in indigo pyjamas, peaked sun hats and armed with old rifles, they raided and ambushed enemy outposts.

Giap taught them to move during rainstorms to deter pursuit, or wade through streams to cover their tracks. He trained them to store supplies, to weave a secret communications web and to eradicate spies and informers. They owed their appeal largely to the fact that they opposed both the French colonial regime and the Japanese occupation army.

From *Vietnam: A History* by Stanley Karnow, Viking Penguin, 1991

Source C Vietminh guerrilla tactics

Independence

By the time of the Japanese surrender in August 1945, Giap and Ho Chi Minh controlled a substantial part of Vietnam. Since the French were still in disarray, Ho Chi Minh took over the rest of the country. On 2 September 1945, speaking into a microphone and surrounded by flags, he announced the formation of the new independent Democratic Republic of Vietnam. He fully expected to get US support and told an American secret service agent he would be delighted to see 'a million American soldiers but not the French'.

The sentiment was not returned. The Americans, who had made it clear during the war that they favoured independence for all colonial peoples, turned back the clock and supported the French and their empire instead. Faced with a choice, the USA supported the anti-Communist forces of France, although this did not reflect popular feeling in Vietnam. The Cold War in Europe had already begun and France was now an important ally in the struggle against worldwide Communism.

Questions

1 Make a list of the events which changed the history of French Indo-China between 1939 and 1945.

2 Use Sources **B** and **C** to explain how the leadership of Ho Chi Minh and General Giap helped the Vietminh fight for the independence of Vietnam.

3 Why did the Vietminh fail to get American support at the end of the war?

4 Design or paint a French poster in 1945 warning people in Indo-China to have nothing to do with Ho Chi Minh and the Vietminh.

5 In no more than 3 or 4 paragraphs, describe the effect the Second World War had on the people of Indo-China.

The war in Indo-China: 1946–54

▶ ## How and why did the French fight a long war against the Vietminh between 1946 and 1954?

The Haiphong incident

The first major confrontation between the Vietminh and the French took place in 1946. An incident in Haiphong harbour on 20 November led to the deaths of 29 French soldiers. The French retaliated by shelling the city from the French warship *Suffren* in the harbour. Over 6,000 Vietnamese civilians and many Vietminh fighters were killed. This set the resolve of Ho Chi Minh and the Nationalists to resist colonial power. The massacre at Haiphong was followed by an equally massive Vietminh act of retaliation in Hanoi three weeks later (Source **B**).

Source A ▶
French Indo-China in the period between 1946 and 1954

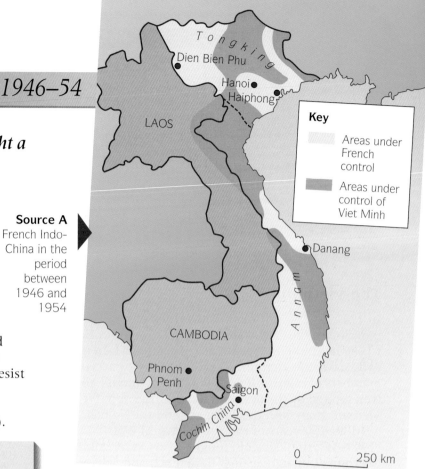

Key

▨ Areas under French control

▧ Areas under control of Viet Minh

0   250 km

Source B
From
The Times,
7 February
1947
▶

Towards 8 p.m. on 10 December 1946 the lights in Hanoi went out. The Annamites [Vietminh] attacked in many parts of the town. A number of French civilians were killed, some with revolting cruelty, and many more were kidnapped. It was a night of terror. Cries for help, the frenzied screaming of the Annamites, grenades exploding and small-arms fire were heard on all sides.

Source C
Saigon,
9 May 1950,
by an
American
journalist in
the city
▶

At sundown, on the city's outskirts, the crump of mortars and occasional rattle of machine guns remind this nerveless city that right on its borders guerrillas are ready to carry out their nocturnal trade.

From *A Long Row of Candles* by C. L. Sulzberger, Macdonald, 1969

The eight-year war

The subsequent war between the French colonial forces and the Vietminh lasted eight years. Using guerrilla tactics (Source **C**, page 5), Giap and his soldiers ambushed convoys and attacked isolated French outposts in the hills and jungles of Vietnam. They usually worked at night. Only rarely did they confront the French forces face to face in battle. As a consequence, they succeeded in controlling large areas of the countryside (Source **A**) while the French remained masters of the cities. But even there they were never far from the fighting (Source **C**).

Source D Until 1949, the Vietminh fought with relatively primitive weapons compared with those equipping the French Army. But Giap made up for their technological shortcomings by using manual labour to move guns, artillery and ammunition. These peasants are trekking southwards carrying weapons for the Vietminh guerrillas in the field.

▶

French rule in Indo-China

In 1949 the French authorities reinstated the Emperor Bao Dai as the puppet ruler of the country, but overall control of the country still lay in the hands of the politicians in Paris. This was not independence – as an Indian politician made plain in 1950 (Source **E**).

Nonetheless, many Vietnamese preferred to be governed by the French. They worked for the government and fought with French armed forces against the Vietminh. Many were Catholics, not Buddhists, and liked to live like Westerners.

Although the French forces were better equipped, they did not yet have all the resources they needed to mount a full-scale military operation in Indo-China. They suffered a further blow in 1949 when Mao Zedong's Communists seized power in China and began training Vietnamese guerrillas and supplying them with modern weapons (Source **F**).

US involvement

Despite assistance from China, the Vietminh were forced back in 1950–51 when General De Lattre de Tassigny inflicted a series of defeats on Vietminh units. The United States had become indirectly involved in the conflict by now: paying for much of the cost of fighting the war. Even this was not enough for the French (Source **G**).

Despite this talk, there was a basic difference between the French and the American attitudes to the war. The French were fighting primarily to preserve their empire. The Americans, who detested imperialism, saw the conflict as a stand against the worldwide spread of Communism and not as a war of independence fought between colonialists and Nationalists. US hardline Secretary of State, John Foster Dulles, told the French: 'If you don't quit, we won't quit.' At the same time, US President Eisenhower refused a French request to send in United States aircraft manned by American crews.

Source E Sir Girja Bajpai's comments to an American journalist

So long as Bao Dai represents a façade it is impossible for real Nationalist Indo-China to support him. We are not champions of Communism but we are champions of Nationalism. If the people of Indo-China want Communism that is their business.

Quoted in *A Long Row of Candles* by C. L. Sulzberger, Macdonald, 1969

Source F Communist China backs the Vietnamese guerrillas

Giap now commanded a real army, backed up by China's enormous weight. A Vietminh officer later said, 'It was a significant moment. We were no longer isolated from the Communist camp.'

From *Vietnam: A History* by Stanley Karnow, Viking Penguin, 1991

Source G By the American journalist, C. L. Sulzberger

Saigon, May 8, 1950: The French feel they are the only fighting force on hand to oppose the extension of dynamic Communism towards South-east Asiatic areas of vast interest to the West. Therefore, they argue the least Washington can do is to make available more equipment and economic aid.

From *A Long Row of Candles* by C. L. Sulzberger, Macdonald, 1969

Questions

1 a) Draw a time chart by putting the following events in chronological order: • Bao Dai restored as Emperor • General De Lattre de Tassigny drives back the Vietminh • French warship shells rebels in Haiphong • Ho Chi Minh declares Vietnam independent • formation of the Vietminh • Red China supplies weapons and trains Vietminh guerrillas • massacre of French citizens in Hanoi.
b) Write brief notes explaining the significance of each event.

2 Use Source **A** to say which areas of Indo-China came under Vietminh control between 1946 and 1954. Why were the Vietminh successful?

3 Use Source **F** and the sources on pages 5 and 6 to describe the advantages the Vietminh guerrillas had compared with the French Army.

4 Why was Bao Dai unacceptable to Asian Nationalists (Source **E**)?

5 What argument did the French use to try to persuade the US government to give them more help?

The Battle of Dien Bien Phu

▶ **What happened at Dien Bien Phu in 1954 and what effect did it have on Indo-China?**

Setting a trap

In 1953 General De Lattre de Tassigny's successor, General Navarre, decided to set a trap. He would tempt General Giap into breaking cover and launching a frontal attack on French positions – only to be wiped out by the superior firepower of the French and their command of the air. He chose the place to do this with care; a junction town on a plateau overlooked by surrounding hills. It was called Dien Bien Phu.

Dien Bien Phu controlled the main routes between Vietnam and the neighbouring regions of Laos and Cambodia. The French built a heavily fortified army base there with an inner ring of strongpoints codenamed Huguette, Françoise, Claudine, Elaine and Dominique. They were protected by three isolated strongpoints to the north (Anne-Marie, Gabrielle and Beatrice) and another, Isabelle, to the south. It was like a medieval castle only the strongpoints were in the valley instead of on the hills.

The Vietminh attack

The French waited for Giap and the Vietminh to attack. But Navarre had made a fatal mistake. He automatically assumed that the Vietminh, with their peasant army on foot and on bicycles, would not be able to move heavy guns into position on the hills surrounding the plateau. But they did.

On 13 March 1954 the siege of Dien Bien Phu began. The Vietminh guerrillas quickly overran the northern stand-alone outposts. Then, from the hills to the east, they directed devastating fire from their guns on the luckless French below.

At the end of March, the inner ring of strongpoints came under attack. The Vietminh advanced in waves, oblivious to casualties, hurling themselves at the French defences (Sources **C** and **D**).

Source A French paratroops land near Dien Bien Phu

Source B Vietminh artillery shells the airfield at Dien Bien Phu

Source C From *Time* magazine, 22 March 1954

▶ To the shrilling of bugles, troops of the Communist Vietminh poured onto a saucerlike plateau in the mountains of Indo-China one day last week and launched a crucial battle of the seven-year Indo-China war. The Communists poured screaming flesh and blood against the French concrete, wire and land mines. Most of the attackers fired rifles, pistols and Tommy guns, but some hurled razor-sharp spears. Wave after wave they came on through the night.

Source D From *Time* magazine, 5 April 1954

▶ Chill mists hung low over besieged Dien Bien Phu, and gecko lizards croaked in the night. From the hills, Communist General Giap's loudspeaker blared at the defenders in Vietnamese, French, Arabic and German: 'Surrender or die.' The 15,000 French Union defenders did not bother to reply.

Victory and defeat

The Vietminh soldiers never faltered. They got their reward on 7 May when Vietminh units broke through the inner ring of strongpoints. Afterwards an American journalist said: 'A deep stillness lay across the wasteland of Dien Bien Phu. A shroud of gunsmoke lifted from the dips and hollows where the French Union garrison had died.' The battle was over.

Source E Last radio telephone call from Brigadier General Christian de Castries to French headquarters

Friday, 7 May 1954. 5.30 p.m. After 20 hours of ceaseless combat, just now man-to-man, the enemy has infiltrated right through our central bastion. Munitions are short. Our resistance is about to be submerged. The Vietminh are only a few yards from the radio where I speak. I have given orders for maximum demolitions. The ammunition depots are going up already. I have just ordered all able-bodied men to go to Isabelle by all means in their power. We can no longer do anything. We will not surrender. Au revoir.

French: 4,000 killed and wounded. 8,000 missing, most captured. North Vietnamese: 8,000 killed, 12,000 wounded.

Source F Statistics of the battle

Omens for the future

The demoralising and humiliating defeat at Dien Bien Phu ended French plans to hold on to Indo-China. They agreed to most of the Vietminh demands at peace talks held later that year in Geneva (pages 10–11).

General Navarre blamed the Americans for not coming to his aid, even though they had already provided huge funds to fight the war. However, when defeat for the French seemed imminent, the American minister responsible for the Far East forecast that the United States would soon become involved – and even predicted the outcome (Source **G**).

Source G A conversation between the US minister in charge of Far East affairs and C. L. Sulzberger

It is impossible for us to lose South-east Asia which would follow the loss of Indo-China. We must intervene. The loss of South-east Asia would not only represent an enormous loss of face, but also of vital raw materials. Yet any kind of war means the end of our civilisation, quite apart from the destructive power of new weapons. Another war would bankrupt the country. But if we are going to intervene we have to intervene wholeheartedly. This is a time to tighten our belts, for unpopular decisions and higher taxes – not for a soft, easy, luxurious life.

Quoted in *A Long Row of Candles* by C. L. Sulzberger, Macdonald, 1969

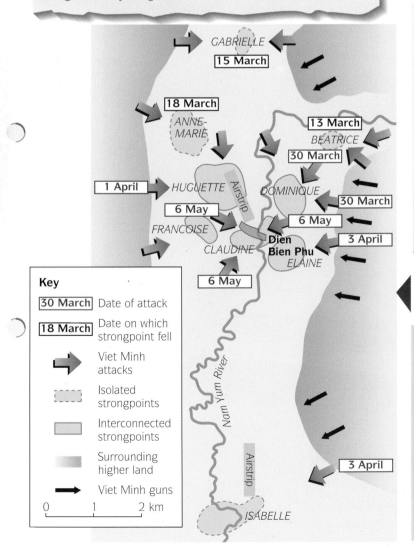

Source H Map of the Battle of Dien Bien Phu in 1954

Key
30 March	Date of attack
18 March	Date on which strongpoint fell
➡	Viet Minh attacks
⬚	Isolated strongpoints
▢	Interconnected strongpoints
▨	Surrounding higher land
→	Viet Minh guns

0   1   2 km

Questions

1 Use the sources on these pages to draw a picture strip telling the story of the Battle of Dien Bien Phu.

2 Use the map (Source **H**) and Sources **C**, **D** and **E** to explain briefly how, when and why the Vietminh defeated the French at Dien Bien Phu.

3 Using the information here and on page 7, list the ways in which the Americans were already involved in Vietnam before the end of May 1954.

2 US involvement in Vietnam: 1954–64

The Geneva Agreement and its effects

▶ *What was the Geneva Agreement and what effect did it have on Vietnam?*

Source A
The signing of the Geneva Agreement

Peace at any price

The defeat at Dien Bien Phu was too much for the French to bear. Peace talks which had already begun in Geneva led to the temporary partition of Vietnam (Source **B**).

Source B The Geneva Agreement

- France to grant independence to Laos, Cambodia and Vietnam.
- Vietnam to be split in half – but only temporarily – by a partition line along the 17th parallel – 17° North.
- A strip of land separating the two Vietnams to become a demilitarized zone (where soldiers were not permitted).
- Free and democratic elections to be held in 1956 under the supervision of an International Control Commission to reunite North and South Vietnam under a single leader.

At the conference the Americans were especially critical of the French and refused to play a leading role in the negotiations. They said the French Prime Minister, Pierre Mendès-France, was a 'peace-at-any-price man'. But an American journalist wrote that however much the US tried to disassociate itself from the Geneva Agreement, 'it was also a defeat for the US'. The South Vietnamese who had fought with the French were disillusioned as well (Source **C**).

Source C By a Vietnamese politician in 1954

We've lost confidence in the French and now we've lost confidence in the Americans and the British. The only place left to put your confidence is with the Communists, and I can't do that.

Quoted in *Time* magazine, 2 August 1954

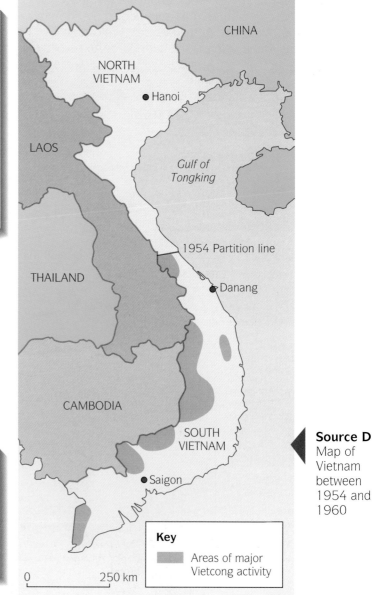

Source D
Map of Vietnam between 1954 and 1960

CHINA

NORTH VIETNAM

● Hanoi

LAOS

Gulf of Tongking

THAILAND

1954 Partition line

● Danang

CAMBODIA

SOUTH VIETNAM

● Saigon

Key

Areas of major Vietcong activity

0   250 km

Neither the US government nor the government of South Vietnam signed the Agreement. However, the US spokesman did say it 'would take a serious view of any violation of an agreed armistice', and pledged to 'refrain from the threat or use of force'. US critics claimed the Agreement had tilted the balance of world power in favour of Communist power. 'While the US looked on, France and England signed over 12 million Vietnamese and half a country to Communism', wrote an American journalist. The South Vietnamese delegate felt likewise and sent a telegram back to Saigon criticising Vietnam's 'false friends' (Source **E**).

The other side of the story

The former Soviet leader, Nikita Khruschev, also suggested that the French and British may have given too much away at Geneva. In his memoirs, he described talks he had had with Chinese Prime Minister, Chou En-Lai, earlier in 1954 (Source **F**).

The agreement left the North in the hands of Ho Chi Minh, and the predominantly Buddhist south under the control of the Emperor Bao Dai. About 80,000 Communist refugees moved north and hundreds of thousands of Catholic refugees moved south.

Free elections?

Ho Chi Minh was confident he would win the elections in 1956 since South Vietnam was ruled by the Emperor Bao Dai, a man associated with the hated French. But Bao Dai appointed Ngo Dinh Diem as Prime Minister of South Vietnam. A year later, Diem repaid this trust by ousting Bao Dai and turning South Vietnam into a republic with himself as President. Diem was a fervent Nationalist supported by the Americans. Ho Chi Minh could no longer be so sure he would win.

Diem, for his part, had no intention of taking the risk. He refused to hold the elections, arguing that the Communists would not allow free elections in the North. He was supported by the US government and US public opinion (Source **G**). They may well have been right. Nonetheless, it was a breach of the Geneva Peace Agreement which the Americans had promised to support if not to defend.

Source G   From *Time* magazine in 1956

South Vietnam rightly argues that no free election could possibly be allowed in the more populous Communist North, and a rigged one would give the Communists a chance to grab the whole country.

WE FOUGHT DESPERATELY AGAINST PARTITION AND FOR A NEUTRAL ZONE IN THE CATHOLIC AREA OF NORTH VIETNAM. ABSOLUTELY IMPOSSIBLE TO OVERCOME THE HOSTILITY OF OUR ENEMIES AND THE TREACHERY OF FALSE FRIENDS.

Quoted in *Time* magazine, 2 August 1954

Source E   South Vietnamese telegram criticising the Agreement

Chou En-Lai took me into a corner. He said: 'Comrade Ho Chi Minh has told me that the situation in Vietnam is hopeless and that if we don't attain a cease-fire soon, the Vietnamese won't be able to hold out against the French.' Then a miracle happened. When the delegations arrived in Geneva for the conference, the Vietminh won a great victory and captured Dien Bien Phu. When France proposed partition along the 17th Parallel, we gasped with surprise and pleasure. We hadn't expected anything like this.

From *Khruschev Remembers* translated by Strobe Talbot, Little, Brown, 1970

Source F   By Nikita Khruschev

Questions

1 Which do you think were the most important terms agreed at Geneva? How did they affect Vietnam?

2 Use the information in the text and the sources to explain why the North Vietnamese were pleased and the South Vietnamese and Americans displeased with the peace settlement.

3 To what extent is Source **G** a fair or biased comment on the elections which both sides agreed to hold in 1956?

4 What additional details does Source **F** add to the information already given here about the position of the Vietminh at the time of the Geneva peace talks? If this assessment was accurate, why were the French unable to see it too?

5 Source **F** is from Nikita Khruschev's memoirs, which were published in the West in 1970. Khruschev denied they were his but many Western experts thought them authentic. What value, if any, is there in using them to understand the position of the Vietminh before and during the Geneva conference?

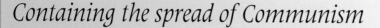

Containing the spread of Communism

▶ *How and why did the Americans become increasingly involved in Vietnam between 1954 and 1964?*

US attitudes to Communism

The United States in the 1950s was obsessed with stopping Communism from spreading. Thousands of American citizens had been accused of being members or supporters of, or sympathisers with, the Communist Party in the USA. Many people had lost their jobs or been hounded out of office. Almost everyone was anti-Communist. Failure to share this view was regarded with suspicion.

US forces had only recently lost 30,000 men fighting for South Korea against Communist China and North Korea. The situation there seemed clearcut. There were bad guys in the North, good guys in the South. Americans assumed the same to be true of North and South Vietnam.

To stop Communism spreading across South-east Asia, the US helped to form the South-East Asia Treaty Organization (SEATO) later in 1954. Its members – Australia, France, New Zealand, Pakistan, the Philippines, Thailand, the UK and the USA – pledged themselves to protect the countries of South-east Asia although only five of them (Australia, New Zealand, the USA, Thailand and the Philippines) later sent troops to Vietnam.

Nhu. He also gave government jobs to his fellow Catholics rather than to the Buddhists who were in the majority.

US advisers in Vietnam

Source A President Eisenhower (extreme left) and John Foster Dulles (second from left) greet Ngo Dinh Diem (second from right) in 1957

Corruption and oppression

Meanwhile Diem's refusal to hold the 1956 elections led to confrontation with the North. Many Vietminh sympathisers still lived in the South. One of Diem's top priorities he said was to 'detect Communist spies left behind by the Vietminh'. He immediately set about crushing his opponents and waging war on Communist sympathisers. The oppressive methods he used to do this and the widespread corruption in his regime turned many people against him. They resented the fact that Diem put his close relatives in positions of power, such as his brother, Ngo Dinh

Until 1959 Vietnam was fairly peaceful. To make doubly sure that the country stayed pro-Western and anti-Communist, the United States poured in economic aid and modern weapons and sent military advisers to South Vietnam. This programme began in November 1954 when President Eisenhower (Source **A**) gave 17 officers sealed orders sending them to Saigon. By January 1961, when Eisenhower left office, the number of advisers had grown to 685. But they were not there to fight. Instead they trained the ARVN (Army of the Republic of Vietnam) in the use of conventional weapons to combat an expected invasion from the North.

The Domino Theory

The US involvement in Vietnam was largely at the insistence of Eisenhower's Secretary of State (Foreign Minister), John Foster Dulles (Source **A**). Dulles, a rigid anti-Communist hardliner, argued that the pro-Western governments of other Asian countries, such as Thailand and Malaya, would fall like dominoes – each one pushing over its neighbour – if any one of them was toppled by the Communists. Most Americans agreed with him (Source **B**).

Source B From *Time* magazine in 1961

If the USA cannot or will not save South Vietnam from the Communist assault, no Asian nation can ever again feel safe in putting its faith in the US – and the fall of all of South-east Asia would only be a matter of time.

Source C Vietcong prisoners captured by the ARVN in 1962. Notice the black 'pyjamas' they wore – like most of the peasants in the country.

It is surprising, however, that the Domino Theory was ever taken seriously in America since the largest domino of all, China, had toppled over in 1949 without causing her neighbours to follow suit. Many people in Europe and the rest of the world disagreed with the Americans. They said the US was wrong to interfere in Vietnam's internal affairs. It was not up to the Americans to say who should, or should not, govern an independent country.

Renewal of the guerrilla campaign

Since the planned reunification of an independent Vietnam had been prevented by Diem and the Americans, the North Vietnamese Communists restarted the guerrilla campaign. About 5,000 Vietminh guerrillas were already in position in South Vietnam in 1959, supported by another 100,000 sympathisers in the countryside.

To supplement these numbers and gain more recruits in the South, they sent many of the 80,000 South Vietnamese refugees back across the border. This time they went as trained soldiers carrying the weapons, ammunition and equipment they needed for a guerrilla war. They made their way along a secret route in the western hills, which was later called the Ho Chi Minh Trail (page 29).

The Vietcong

As their strength increased, the Communists in the South formed the National Front for the Liberation of South Vietnam in December 1960. Diem and the Americans dismissed the NLF with contempt, calling its members the Vietcong ('Vietnamese Communists'). By 1961, there were 20,000 Vietcong guerrillas in the South. By 1964, they had grown to over 100,000 and operated at will in Vietnam's jungles, forested hills and swamps. Neither Diem's police, nor the ARVN, had been adequately trained to deal with guerrilla warfare. To the dismay of the Americans, the Vietcong created turmoil and seemed to be winning the war.

This is why the new US President, John F. Kennedy (a Democrat), secretly increased the number of US 'advisers' in Vietnam. By November 1963, when Lyndon B. Johnson took over as US President, the number had grown from 685 in 1961 to 16,000.

Questions

1 Which US president first involved the USA in Vietnam? What was his main reason for doing so?

2 Which US president first began the rapid escalation of US involvement in the conflict? What was his main reason for doing so?

3 Use the sources and the information in the text to write a short account explaining why American soldiers were sent to Vietnam.

4 What right had the Americans to expect the people of Vietnam to support a pro-Western government? Discuss this with members of your class.

Ngo Dinh Diem

▶ *Why was Ngo Dinh Diem assassinated and what effect did this have on Vietnam and the course of the war?*

Strategic hamlets

Despite everything, the Americans failed to establish an effective and popular pro-Western government in South Vietnam. The strategic hamlet programme, for instance, proved a costly failure. Officials fortified selected villages which they thought could be most easily defended against the Vietcong. Then villagers for miles around were sent to live in them. As you can see from Source **A**, the policy was very unpopular with the Vietnamese.

Mounting opposition

Ngo Dinh Diem also antagonised the peasants by putting government officials from the cities, who knew nothing about peasant life and its traditions, in charge of the countryside. Many farmers even lost the land they had gained under the Vietminh before 1954.

There was also growing opposition as Diem continued to favour Roman Catholics at the expense of Buddhists. The issue flared up again in the summer of 1963 when the Catholics of the northern city of Hué were given permission to fly religious flags in honour of their Archbishop (Ngo Dinh Diem's brother). But similar permission was later refused to Buddhists wanting to fly flags on the Buddha's birthday. Street protests followed and nine Buddhists were killed in May.

The controversy aroused worldwide anger when a Buddhist monk, drenched in petrol, set himself on fire in June. The Buddhists made sure they got maximum press coverage by alerting the world's press well in advance (Sources **B** and **C**).

Source A By the Labour politician Denis Healey, after visiting a strategic hamlet in 1964

The Americans persuaded the Vietnam government to herd the peasants into 'strategic hamlets'. It was a disaster. Peasants should never be taken more than five miles from the land they farm. The hamlets were heavily infiltrated by the Vietcong. Of eight thousand only one thousand were judged secure.

From *The Time of My Life* by Denis Healey, Michael Joseph, 1989

Source B A Buddhist monk in flames – a gruesome but effective protest against the repressive policies of Ngo Dinh Diem

Source C
From *The Mass Media War* by Dennis J. Duncanson

They staged the first suicide by an elderly monk for the pressmen to record. The impact was impressive. The prize-winning photograph of saffron-robed Father 'Spreading Virtue' engulfed in yellow and scarlet flames, published all over the United States and the world, changed the course of Vietnamese history.

Quoted in *History of the 20th Century*, Purnell, 1970

US disillusionment with Diem

US President John F. Kennedy was deeply affected by the image of the burning Buddhist monk. He became increasingly reluctant to support the Diem regime (Sources **D** and **E**).

Source E News report in *The Times*, 3 September 1963

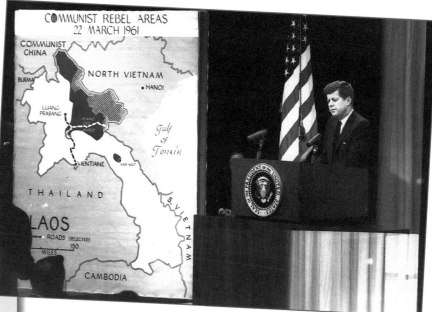

Source D President Kennedy at a press conference

Washington, 2 September 1963: President Kennedy said tonight that he did not think the war against the Communists in South Vietnam could be won unless a greater effort was made by the government of President Ngo Dinh Diem to win popular support. Mr Kennedy also announced that the United States was prepared to continue providing assistance to the South Vietnam government, although he thought 'the repressions against Buddhists in the country were very unwise'.

In desperation, Diem sought popularity by trying to keep down the number of casualties sustained by the South Vietnamese army. Officers were criticised if they attacked the enemy. This further antagonised the Americans, who were picking up the bill (Source **F**).

Source F Attitude of US war correspondents to Diem in 1963

Why should the United States have already forfeited 50 American lives and more than $400,000,000 for a corrupt government, a South Vietnamese army that would not fight, and a nation in chaos, where the guerrillas ruled the countryside and the people hated the government? Either the US should get out, or the US should take control and win this war.

From *The Complete Military History of the Vietnam War* by Douglas Welsh, Brompton Books, 1990

The assassination of Ngo Dinh Diem

Two months later came the shock news that Diem and his much-hated brother and political adviser, Ngo Dinh Nhu, had been assassinated by ARVN officers worried the Americans would withdraw their support if Diem continued in power. The US authorities knew about the plot beforehand but did nothing to prevent it (Source **G**).

For weeks – and with the President informed every step of the way – the American mission in Saigon maintained secret contacts with the plotting generals through one of the Central Intelligence Agency's most experienced and versatile operators.

Source G By Hedrick Smith in *The New York Times*, 1 July 1971

It was yet another 'disastrous turning point' for Vietnam since Diem's successors were no more successful than he had been in controlling the country. But American acceptance of Diem's murder did little for their cause. Ironically, President Kennedy himself was assassinated only three weeks later.

Questions

1 Using the sources and information in this chapter, explain why support for the Vietcong increased sharply between 1960 and 1964.

2 What was wrong with the strategic hamlets according to Denis Healey (Source **A**)?

3 Use Sources **E** and **F** to make a list of American complaints about Ngo Dinh Diem.

4 Look at the photograph of the Buddhist monk in flames (Source **B**). Why do you think it made such an impact on the West?

5 What part did Ngo Dinh Diem play in the Vietnam crisis? What effect did his assassination have on the conflict?

6 Draw up a time chart listing the main events in the history of Vietnam from 1939 to 1964.

Escalating the war: 1964–67

The Gulf of Tongking incident

▶ *How did US policy in South Vietnam change in the three years between 1964 and 1967 and with what results?*

A new president

When US President Lyndon B. Johnson first came to office in November 1963, he knew very little about Vietnam and its problems. In March 1964, he asked his top advisers what he should do:

1 Negotiate a settlement with the North;
2 'Send in the Marines' (go all-out for victory);
3 'Continue our present policy' (of maintaining a force of advisers);
4 'Come out now and let the dominoes fall?'

At first, he chose option 3 and continued to send military advisers to Vietnam. By May 1964, however, he had come to the conclusion that Vietnam was 'the biggest damn mess I ever saw'. He told a senior adviser: 'I don't think it's worth fighting for and I don't think we can get out.' In the next few months, he secretly altered course. He took America in a new and dangerous direction, the first news of which exploded in headlines on 5 August 1964 (Source **B**).

Source A Map of the Vietnam war 1964–67

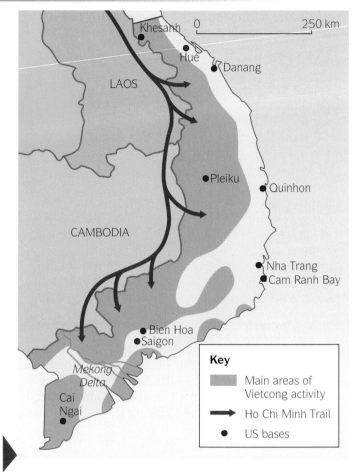

Key

- Main areas of Vietcong activity
- Ho Chi Minh Trail
- US bases

Source B Headlines in *The New York Times*, 5 August 1964

US PLANES ATTACK NORTH VIETNAM BASES:
PRESIDENT ORDERS 'LIMITED' RETALIATION AFTER
COMMUNISTS' TORPEDO BOATS RENEW RAIDS

REDS DRIVEN OFF

Two Torpedo Vessels Believed Sunk in Gulf of Tongking

The incident in the Gulf of Tongking was only an excuse. Johnson and his advisers greatly exaggerated a minor incident off the coast of North Vietnam – involving a US destroyer which was spying on the North Vietnamese – to persuade Congress (the US parliament) to pass the Gulf of Tongking Resolution giving him the authority 'to take all necessary measures to repel any armed attack against the forces of the United States and to prevent further aggression'.

The attack on Pleiku

Nonetheless, Johnson, a very clever politician, trod carefully. He wanted the full support of the American electorate before driving ahead with plans to defeat the Vietcong and the North Vietnamese Army (NVA). In December 1964, he agreed that US warplanes should bomb the Ho Chi Minh Trail in Laos but refused to let them bomb North Vietnam until he felt he could justify it to the American people.

His justification came on 6–7 February 1965 after the Vietcong attacked the US base at Pleiku (Sources **C** and **D**). Ten aircraft at the base were destroyed, eight US 'advisers' were killed and over a hundred others wounded.

Source C

Damage at the US base at Pleiku in February 1965

Source D A news report in *Newsweek*, 22 February 1965

Guerrillas hiding in a hamlet 1,000 yards from the camp fired mortar bombs smack into the compound where 400 US advisers lived. Seven Americans died, more than 100 were wounded, and nearly a score of aircraft were damaged or destroyed.

Quoted in *The History of the Vietnam War* by Charles T. Kamps Jr, Hamlyn, 1988

Operation Rolling Thunder

US public opinion was outraged. Johnson now had the excuse he needed to call up troops and bomb the North. Operation Rolling Thunder began on 11 February 1965 with a joint attack by US and ARVN warplanes on key military and industrial targets in North Vietnam, such as bridges, railway lines, roads, army barracks and supply depots. Air force officers were confident now that they could end the war. However, their targets were restricted. Air crews were not yet allowed to bomb Hanoi and Haiphong, North Vietnam's biggest cities, for fear of jeopardising US relations with the Soviet Union (Source **E**). Even so, bombing North Vietnam for the first time was a grave and very serious escalation of the war. The President gave three reasons for the bombing campaign (Source **F**).

Operation Rolling Thunder led eventually to an extensive war from the air (pages 20–21). It became the principal weapon used by President Johnson to try to force the North Vietnamese to talk about peace.

The 'Americanization' of the war

Soon afterwards, 3,500 US Marines were sent to the air base at Danang to protect it against guerrilla attacks like the one at Pleiku. This time there was no pretence of calling them 'advisers'. The Marines went to South Vietnam as US soldiers prepared to fight a war. From this moment on, the Americans took control of the South Vietnamese war effort with direction of military operations firmly in the hands of Lieutenant-General William Westmoreland, the top American commander in Vietnam. In a matter of months, many more troops arrived in South Vietnam as well, including soldiers from Australia and New Zealand.

In December 1964, there were 16,000 US troops in South Vietnam (Source **I** on page 18). Two years later, this total had rocketed to 268,000 and in January 1968 it reached a peak of well over 500,000. So much, then, for President Johnson's earlier promise to the American people (Source **H**).

The result of the self-imposed restrictions of Rolling Thunder was that large safe areas were created which protected 80 per cent of North Vietnam's industry and 75 per cent of its population.

From *The History of the Vietnam War* by Charles T. Kamps Jr, Hamlyn, 1988

Source E
The limitations of the bombing campaign

To increase the confidence of the brave people of South Vietnam, to convince the leaders of North Vietnam that we will not be defeated, and to reduce the flow of men and supplies from the North.

From *To Seek a Newer World* by Robert F. Kennedy, Michael Joseph, 1968

Source F
President Johnson's reasons for bombing North Vietnam

Source G An American F4 Phantom II fighter over the South China Sea in October 1965

We are not about to send American boys nine or ten thousand miles away from home to do what Asian boys ought to be doing for themselves.

Source H
By President Johnson

Questions

1 How and why did President Johnson increase American involvement in Vietnam in 1964–65?

2 Look at the map (Source **A**). What do you notice about the following:
   a) The position of the US bases on the map?
   b) The position of the Ho Chi Minh Trail?

3 What was Operation Rolling Thunder and how did it mark a change in the direction of the war?

Source I US servicemen in Vietnam 1962–72

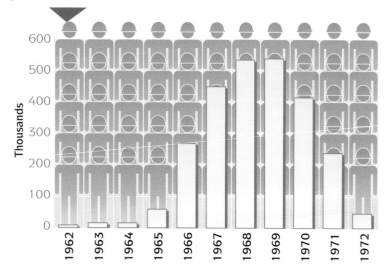

US policy and the war on land

Despite the rapid growth of US armed forces in Vietnam, the Vietcong continued to increase its hold on the countryside. They were joined by regular soldiers from the NVA who began to infiltrate the South in 1965. The NVA fought in larger units than the Vietcong leaving the guerrillas to wage a terrorist war of ambush and murder. But, for three years, they suffered a number of substantial defeats at the hands of the US armed forces.

In August 1965, US Marines involved in Operation Star Light won an important victory over the NVA to the south of Danang. US forces also defeated them at the Battle of Plei Me in October and again in November when the US First Cavalry won a major battle at Iadrang on the Cambodian border.

Search and destroy missions

In 1966 the Americans began a series of search and destroy missions (pages 30–31) to hunt down NVA units and the Vietcong. In order to mount these operations, a number of huge supply bases had been built at the coast, such as at Danang and Cam Ranh Bay (page 16). These supported the smaller 'firebases' built inland (page 23) which were supplied by helicopter and from which the search and destroy units went out on patrol. Increasingly, helicopters rather than armoured personnel carriers were used to carry troops into battle (page 25). Much of the ground in Vietnam was jungle, swamp or paddy field and soon proved unsuitable for tanks (pages 24–25).

One of the largest of these missions, Operation Junction City, took place in February 1967 to the north of Saigon (Source **K**).

Source J   US radio operator Charles H. Richey of the 1st Cavalry Division on patrol in May 1968

After swarms of low-flying jets had softened up the landing zone with rockets and machine-gun fire, wave after wave of helicopters fluttered in over the treetops, landing and disgorging thousands of US infantrymen. In the very middle of the zone, the sky was alive with paratroopers, and from the outskirts of the zone thousands more US and ARVN troops closed in. Operation Junction City, the biggest US offensive of the war to date, was under way.

Quoted in *The History of the Vietnam War* by Charles T. Kamps Jr, Hamlyn, 1988

Source K   Operation Junction City, 22 February 1967

Once again, a major operation ended in victory for US forces. By now, General Westmoreland (Source **M**) was convinced the war could be won this way (Source **L**).

> North Vietnam is paying a tremendous price with nothing to show for it in return. The war is not a stalemate. We are winning, slowly but steadily.
>
> Quoted in *Time* magazine, 14 July 1967

Source M Lieutenant-General William Westmoreland (extreme right) with US Defense Secretary Robert McNamara (centre) and leading officers from the ARVN

Pacification

Right at the outset, however, the Americans realised that their search and destroy operations could lose them the confidence and trust of civilians caught up in the fighting. This is why they introduced a policy called 'pacification'. It was designed to 'win the hearts and minds' of the people of South Vietnam.

Rehousing refugees, providing clinics and schools and bringing in elections to local offices were important parts of this policy. Pacification teams also helped peasants to build new roads, bridges, canals and drainage ditches. They encouraged villagers to set up self-help groups to improve methods of farming.

Unfortunately the time, energy and money spent on the pacification programme took second place to the need to wipe out the Vietcong and the NVA units which had infiltrated the South. Nonetheless, the scheme had some success. When the Communists mounted their full-scale Tet Offensive in 1968 (page 38), the South Vietnamese, as a whole, showed little enthusiasm for a Communist revolution.

Creating a democracy

Meanwhile, American efforts to create a more democratic society in South Vietnam met with far less success. When a South Vietnamese student was asked in 1968 what he wanted most for his country, he replied: 'Do away with corruption and nepotism and, if you can, give more freedom to the people.'

After the assassination of Ngo Dinh Diem in 1963, the country was ruled briefly by a number of short-lived governments until Air Vice-Marshal Nguyen Cao Ky became Prime Minister in June 1965, with General Nguyen Van Thieu as Head of State. Elections to a new parliament were held in 1966 and a constitution was drawn up and approved. When a presidential election was held in September 1967, however, there was little change at the top. Nguyen Van Thieu became President and Nguyen Cao Ky was elected Vice-President.

The policy of attrition

As the war progressed, US forces suffered many casualties, but these were always small compared with those suffered by the Vietcong and the NVA. This is why General Westmoreland thought he could win a war of attrition (page 22). This is where one side wins by killing more of the enemy's men than he can afford to lose. Although this may have made sense to US Army commanders, it didn't make sense to the average citizen back home in the USA. Attrition could only work as a policy if the US public was prepared to accept the losses it would entail. As you will see (pages 42–45), this was very far from being the case.

Questions

1 List the following events in chronological order, adding the relevant date or year:
   • Operation Rolling Thunder • Operation Junction City • the assassination of Ngo Dinh Diem • the Gulf of Tongking incident • the attack on Pleiku • Operation Star Light • Nguyen Van Thieu elected President.
   Add a brief note to each event on your list explaining its importance in the war.

2 Look at the bar chart (Source **I**). Between which two or three years did the strength of US armed forces in Vietnam grow most rapidly? When did it fall? In which year was American involvement in Vietnam at its peak?

3 What part did the NVA play in the war
   a) before 1964?
   b) between 1964 and 1967?

4 What did the US armed forces try to achieve in Vietnam in 1964–67?

The war in the air

▶ *What effect did the war in the air have on the conflict?*

Targeting the North

The US warplanes which bombed North Vietnam came from three types of air base:

1 US bases in South Vietnam itself, such as at Danang;
2 US aircraft carriers patrolling the waters off the coast of North Vietnam (Source **A**);
3 US air bases in Thailand and the Pacific island of Guam.

The last-named bases had the facilities needed by the giant B-52 bombers (Source **D**) which brought terror to the North.

In fact, the air raids in the first six months made very little impact. Restricting the targets which could be bombed was not a success. The flow of men and materials from the North continued to grow. More and more targets were added to the list, such as bridges, railway lines, supply dumps and oil installations but many were difficult targets to hit (Source **B**).

Source A US aircraft carrier *Enterprise* in the Gulf of Tongking off the coast of North Vietnam in 1966

could neither be seen nor heard from the ground. Each bomber carried 28 bombs weighing two tonnes apiece. All told, they dropped three times as much explosive on Vietnam as was dropped on Germany and Japan during the whole of the Second World War. You can see what effect they had in Source **C**.

Source B By James Cameron, a British war correspondent in North Vietnam in December 1965

The famous Ham Rong bridge has been attacked more than 100 times, by at least 1,000 aircraft. It is scarred and pitted and twisted and the area around is a terrible mess, but the bridge still carries the road and railroad. It lies between two very steep hills and must be extremely difficult to hit. It would need a very steep and oblique bombing run.

Quoted in *The Faber Book of Reportage* edited by John Carey, 1987

Source C From the *Journal of a Vietcong* by Truong Nhu Tang

From a kilometre away, the sonic roar of the B-52 explosions tore ear drums, leaving many of the jungle dwellers permanently deaf. From a kilometre, the shock waves knocked their victims senseless. Any hit within a half kilometre would collapse the walls of an unreinforced bunker, burying alive the people cowering inside. Seen up close, the bomb craters were gigantic – thirty feet [9 metres] across and nearly as deep.

Quoted in *The Bloody Game: An Anthology of Modern War* edited by Paul Fussell, Scribners, 1991

Source D US B-52 bombers dropping bombs on North Vietnam

Saturation bombing

As the war intensified, however, selective targeting was replaced by saturation (blanket) bombing – trying to bomb the North Vietnamese to the conference table by dropping bombs on everything in sight. The giant B-52 bombers were first used for this purpose in April 1966 (Source **D**). These huge planes flew at over 15,000 metres high (50,000 feet). They

Pilots with Soviet Mig-21 fighters

Surface-to-air missiles

Anti-aircraft gunners

One-man air-raid shelters

Heavy machine guns

Effects on North Vietnamese morale

In the long run, the air raids – like those on London in 1940–41 – only strengthened the determination of the North Vietnamese to resist (Source **E**).

The area surrounding Hanoi and Haiphong soon became 'the most heavily defended region the world has ever seen'. As a consequence, many American pilots and aircrew were killed or taken prisoner of war. Between 1965 and 1968, over 1,400 US warplanes were shot down over North Vietnam.

The North Vietnamese used three main methods to combat the incoming American bombers (Source **F**):

1 Anti-aircraft guns. These were manned by eager gun crews who shot down most of the US warplanes crashing in North Vietnam.
2 Surface-to-air missiles (SAM) supplied by the Soviet Union. These electronic devices were actually less effective than the older anti-aircraft guns – largely because the American pilots were able to use counter-measures to evade the oncoming missiles.
3 Soviet Mig-17 and Mig-21PF fighters armed with air-to-air missiles. Many of the North Vietnamese pilots were highly skilled and well-respected by their American counterparts.

In the centre of Hanoi the authorities erected a huge sign to keep up people's spirits (Source **G**).

Source F
By a North Vietnamese doctor, Ton That Tung, after the war

The Americans thought that the more bombs they dropped, the quicker we would fall to our knees and surrender. But the bombs heightened rather than dampened our spirit.

Quoted in *Vietnam: A History* by Stanley Karnow, Viking Penguin, 1991

Questions

1 What reasons lay behind President Johnson's refusal to allow US warplanes to bomb Hanoi and Haiphong in 1965?

2 Use a school atlas map of South-east Asia to draw your own map of Vietnam and its neighbours to show Thailand, Guam, the Philippines, Laos, Cambodia, Hanoi and Saigon. Add labels saying why each place played an important part in the history of Vietnam at this time.

3 To what do you think each of the following quotations refer? Write notes explaining your answer for the benefit of someone who knows nothing about these events.
a) 'In the rainy season they would fill up with water and often saw service as duck or fishponds.'
b) 'Will this sort of thing blow Communism out of their heads?'

4 Write a brief account explaining under sub-headings how the North Vietnamese defended their country from air attack.

5 What did the Americans hope to accomplish by bombing North Vietnam? What did they achieve?

On a big billboard in the city centre, the number of US planes shot down is revised forward almost daily in red paint – 2,818, they claimed when I left, and the number keeps growing. In villages, the score is kept on a blackboard.

Hanoi by Mary McCarthy, 1968

Source G Keeping count of US planes shot down

4 How the war was fought

A war with no front line

▶ **How did the US armed forces fight a war without a front line?**

War aims of the US forces in Vietnam

The main war aim of the US and ARVN forces was to rid South Vietnam of the Vietcong. The US Army High Command made it clear that counting the number of Vietcong killed would define the success or failure of an operation. This was called the body count (Source **B**). It was part of the war of attrition (page 19).

Source A A Chinook helicopter moving a gun into position during a search and destroy mission in September 1967

Our mission was not to win ground or seize positions, but simply to kill. To kill Communists and kill as many of them as possible. Stack 'em up like cordwood. Victory was a high body count, defeat a low kill ratio, war a matter of arithmetic. The pressure on unit commanders to produce enemy corpses was intense and led to such practices as counting civilians as Vietcong. 'If it's dead and Vietnamese, it's Vietcong' was a rule of thumb in the jungle.

From *A Rumor of War* by Philip Caputo, Ballantine, 1968

Source B By a Marine lieutenant

But no matter how many were killed, the Vietcong kept on coming, many of them new recruits – reluctant or willing converts to the Vietcong cause. It soon became clear that the body count was having little apparent effect on Vietcong or North Vietnamese morale. They were always far readier to accept huge losses than either the ARVN (page 52) or the USA (pages 42–43). This fact alone ensured the Communists would triumph in the end. Ho Chi Minh explained why (Source **C**).

Yet the ARVN and the US armed forces had no other effective way of measuring their success. There was no Vietcong territory to invade and conquer, so they could never claim to have advanced so many kilometres or to have captured an important enemy town or fort. US patrols destroyed and burned villages if they sheltered Vietcong. When they departed, they left no one behind to hold on to the territory they had devastated – but they did leave behind hatred for the USA (Source **D**).

Source C
By Ho Chi Minh

You may kill ten of my men for every one I kill of yours. But even at those odds, you will lose and I will win.

Quoted in *The Dictionary of War Quotations* by Jonathan Wintle, Hodder and Stoughton, 1989

Nguyen Bat was not a Communist at the time of the massacre, but the incident changed his mind. 'After the shooting,' he said, 'all the villagers became Communists.'

From *My Lai 4* by Seymour M. Hersh, 1973

Source D After the My Lai massacre in 1968

Strategy

Since they were fighting on their homeland, the Vietcong could afford to wait years for victory. The Americans could not. The colossal cost of fighting the war ($133 billion) meant the US Army was always under pressure to win quickly. By contrast, Ho Chi Minh and the Communists could afford to wait. There was no need to confront the enemy in battle. In time, the Americans would grow tired of the war and go away.

Because there was no front line separating the enemy from US/ARVN forces, General Westmoreland had to devise a way of dealing with the enemy. He decided to set up a system of large, heavily fortified supply bases at the coast. Some of these, such as Danang in the north and Cam Ranh Bay in the south, were as large as a small town with an airport, 100 kilometres or so of roads, and a harbour so they could be reinforced from the sea. Other major bases, heavily fortified and defended, were built at Pleiku and Khesanh (see map on page 16).

The main supply bases supported the smaller fire support bases (Sources **E** and **F**) which acted as local strongholds from which army units went out on search and destroy missions to hunt down the Vietcong.

Source E   An American fire support base

Source F   From *And A Hard Rain Fell* by John Ketwig, published in 1985

The firebase was a hole in the sea of vegetation. Like the eye of a hurricane, a clearing, a grassy meadow had been ringed with barbed wire and sandbags. Near the centre, two big guns hunkered down into the soft mud. M-60 machine guns and automatic rifles stood ready at the perimeter, perched on sandbagged bunkers.

Questions

1 Use Sources **E** and **F** to describe an American firebase. What part did it play in the war?

2 Why was the war fought without a front line? What effect did this have on US war aims?

3 Use Source **B** to say in what circumstances the members of a patrol could return to their fire support base confident their mission had been a success.

4 'The conventional army loses if it does not win, the guerrilla wins if he does not lose.' How did Dr Kissinger's comment apply to the war in Vietnam?

The geography of Vietnam

▶ *How did the geography of Vietnam affect the way in which the war was fought?*

Mountains

Tropical rainforest

Source A

The helicopter war

As you can see from the illustrations and the extracts on these pages, the war in Vietnam was fought under tropical conditions: in the swamps and paddy fields of the south and the hilly jungles of the west and north (Sources **C** to **I**). Because the geography of Vietnam was very different from the type of landscape where most of the soldiers had been trained, it took time for the Army to make good use of the conditions, unlike the Vietcong and NVA fighting on their home soil.

As the war progressed, the Americans made increasing use of helicopters to overcome transport problems on the ground, such as thick rainforest or swamp. They used helicopters as gunships armed with rocket launchers and machine guns. Soldiers took to the air much as their predecessors had gone into battle on horseback hundreds of years earlier (Source **B**).

After a light lunch last Wednesday, General James F. Hollingsworth, of the US 'Big Red I' Division, took off in his personal helicopter and killed more Vietnamese than any of the troops he was commanding. 'There's no better way to fight than goin' out to shoot VCs. An' there's nothing I love better than killin' Cong. No, sir.'

From *The Sunday Times*, 5 June 1966

Source B
By Nicholas Tomalin, a British war correspondent

Last month for the first time in the Vietnamese war, a US infantry battalion waded briefly into the labyrinthian mangrove swamps, coconut groves, and mud flats of the Mekong River Delta. The whole operation was mainly an experiment to see how the American troops would cope with the treacherous, watery terrain that has long been one of the Vietcong's principal strongholds.

Source C From *Time* magazine, 26 November 1965

Source D
The tropical conditions in Vietnam

The heat and rain and insects were almost worse than the enemy. Drenched in sweat, the men waded through flooded paddies and plantations, stopping from time to time to pick leeches out of their boots.

From *Vietnam: A History* by Stanley Karnow, Viking Penguin, 1991

Helicopters were also used as troop carriers (Source **A** on page 30) and as heavy goods vehicles moving guns, vehicles, ammunition, supplies and even boats across swamps, jungles and hills (Source **A** on page 22). The 'choppers' played a dominant role in the search and destroy missions used to hunt down the Vietcong. When a patrol went into action, a fleet of helicopters moved them rapidly into position while helicopter gunships and other war planes sprayed the ground with rockets and machine gun fire (Source **K** on page 18). By the end of the war, the Americans had lost well over 2,200 helicopters in battle.

Source E
A US patrol boat in Vietnam. In the Mekong Delta in the south, boats were often the only effective means of travel.

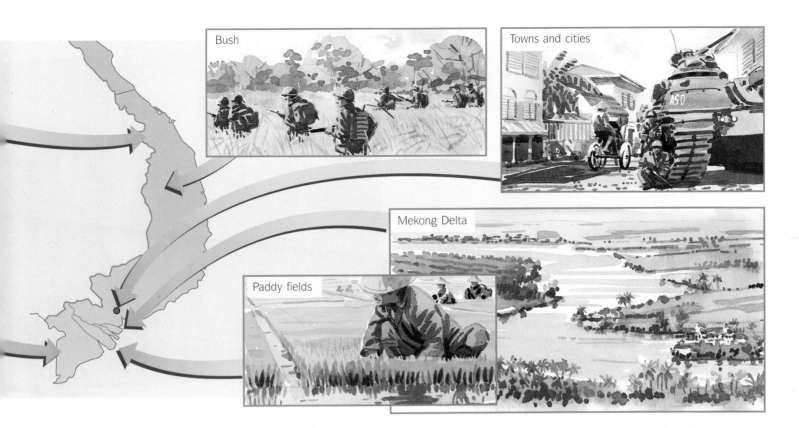

Bush

Towns and cities

Mekong Delta

Paddy fields

Source F From *Time* magazine, 26 November 1965

It is terrible country for fighting. The jungle trees and vines that cover the sharp ridges and deep valleys in the mountains make military movement difficult. Bombs explode harmlessly on the thick jungle canopy.

The Highlands of Vietnam are spooky, unbearably spooky, spooky beyond belief. They are a run of erratic mountain ranges, gnarled valleys, jungled ravines and abrupt plains.

From *Dispatches* by Michael Herr, Picador, 1978

Source H
By a war correspondent

Source G The Americans made more use of the armoured personnel carrier than the tank. The M113 shown here was fast, could travel in water as well as on land, and gave ample protection to the crew when they came under attack from small arms fire.

As we walked, the rains, typical for that time of year, poured down continuously, turning the red Cambodian earth to a sticky clay. We shuffled ahead in the ankle-deep mud. Like robots, we made our way through the downpour. For five days it rained without letup.

From the *Journal of a Vietcong* by Truong Nhu Tang (with David Chanoff and Doan Van Toai), Random, 1985.

Source I
By a Vietcong

Questions

1 What do the sources tell you about Vietnam as a place in which to fight a guerrilla war?

2 How and why did helicopters rather than tanks play such a large part in American operations in the field?

3 Use the sources on these pages to write an account describing how the geography of Vietnam affected the way in which the war was fought.

The Vietcong

> ### Why did the Communists use guerrilla tactics against the US/ARVN forces?

Who were the Vietcong?

The Vietcong (VC for short) were recruited from men and women who lived in, or had fled from, South Vietnam. They were not the same as the North Vietnamese Army (NVA), recruited from people living in the North. The Vietcong fought a guerrilla war, much of it at night (Source **B**). NVA units were trained to fight conventional battles as well.

Source A Vietcong soldiers

Every night furtive [crafty] little bands of Communist guerrillas, dressed in black peasant pyjamas or faded khakis, splash through the marshes of the Mekong Delta or dart silently along jungle paths of South Vietnam, pursuing their intent, murderous missions.

From *Time* magazine, 24 November 1961

Source B By an American journalist in 1961

Friend or foe?

Because the Vietcong did not wear uniform, US and ARVN soldiers on patrol had great difficulty in distinguishing them from peasants working in the fields. Both wore the same black pyjamas and wide straw hats (Source **C**).

Source C By a soldier who served in Vietnam

You never knew who was the enemy and who was the friend. They all looked alike. They all dressed alike. They were all Vietnamese. Some of them were Vietcong.

Quoted in *Vietnam: A History* by Stanley Karnow, 1983

Tactics

1 Initial stages

Infiltrate the countryside, get to know the people, gain their trust, spread the idea of revolution, sign up new recruits.

2 Guerrilla war

a) Ambush enemy vehicles and isolated units

b) Sabotage and terrorism and murder.

c) Plant mines and booby traps.

3 Open warfare

Employ guns, tanks and regular army units to fight set-piece battles.

Source D Vietcong tactics

You can see the three stages of conflict adopted by the Vietcong and NVA in Source **D**.

1 It began with the infiltration of the countryside as the guerrillas merged with the people and gained their support. If kindness didn't work, they used terrorism to get their way – torturing and murdering officials and executing spies (Source **E**).

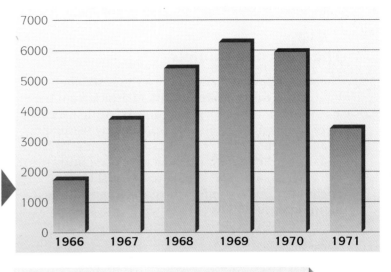

Source E
The number of civilians murdered by the Vietcong

In general, the Vietcong concentrated their forces in the countryside, leaving the cities mainly in government hands. But they were active there as well, as saboteurs and terrorists. They disrupted life and work in Saigon, the capital city, and even inside the US bases. Acts of sabotage reminded everyone why the war was being fought (Sources **F** and **G**).

Source F   By a war correspondent serving in Vietnam

The VC got work inside all the camps as shoeshine boys and laundresses. They'd starch your uniform and then go home and mortar your area.

From Dispatches by Michael Herr, Picador, 1978

Source G
By an Army officer in Vietnam

What's a civilian? Somebody who works for us at day and puts on Vietcong pyjamas at night.

From My Lai 4, by Seymour M. Hersh, 1973

2 Once established in the countryside, the Vietcong began a guerrilla campaign – using small units to attack the US and ARVN forces. They avoided the large-scale face-to-face confrontations they knew they couldn't win. Instead they resorted to ambush, tricks and traps, disguise and camouflage, and attacks on isolated camps and enemy units (Source **H**).

We walk through the mines, trying to catch the Vietcong Forty-eighth Battalion. But he finds us far more often than we do him. He is hidden among the mass of civilians or in tunnels or in jungles. And each piece of ground left behind is his from the moment we are gone on our next hunt.

From If I Die in a Combat Zone by Tim O'Brien, 1973

Source H
By a soldier who served in Vietnam

When chased or hunted, they had an uncanny knack of merging into the landscape (Source **I**).

I've never seen anybody better camouflaged. Once somebody yelled 'There they go!' and all I could see were seven bushes running along the paddy wall about 50 yards away.

Quoted in The History of the Vietnam War by Charles T. Kamps Jr, Hamlyn, 1988

Source I
By an American soldier

3 Conventional warfare – fighting in large formations and using tanks and heavy artillery – was only used when circumstances allowed. NVA units often fought this way (pages 38–39) but they were just as skilled as the Vietcong at disguising their presence and vanishing into thin air (Source **J**).

When the hideous Battle of Dak To ended at the top of Hill 875, we announced that 4,000 of them had been killed. It had been the purest slaughter, our losses were bad, but clearly it was another American victory. But when the top of the hill was reached, the number of NVA found was four. Four. Of course more died, hundreds more, but the corpses counted and photographed and buried numbered four. Where, Colonel? And how, and why? All that terrain, all of that cover, ridge after ridge, murderous slides and gorges, all cloaked by forest and thick monsoon mists. And whole divisions [of the NVA] were out there in that.

From Dispatches by Michael Herr, Picador, 1978

Source J   The NVA used the landscape as cover

Questions

1 Look at Source **D**. Why was it important for the Vietcong to infiltrate the villages and get to know the people?

2 Use the sources on these pages to explain how the Vietcong were skilled at merging with the landscape in which they fought.

The Vietcong tunnels

The American command of the air exposed the Vietcong to the ever-present risk of attack from the air. To counter this, they dug tunnels. At first they were simple dugouts to hide from enemy warplanes or a place from which to ambush the enemy. By the end of the war, the tunnels had developed into an extensive system, 250 kilometres in total length. There were underground kitchens, weapons stores, dormitories, hospitals and rest areas. US soldiers at the time saw the Vietcong tunnels as proof of their own success – the Vietcong had been forced to hide underground. But was there another way of looking at it?

Interpreting the tunnels

In 1993, Channel 4 televised a programme in which Julian Pettifer, a former BBC war correspondent, went back to Vietnam after 25 years to reassess the war. He described his reaction to the Vietcong tunnels (Source **L**).

Source L Julian Pettifer speaking on Channel 4, 27 June 1993

The American story was that this was an example of the success of their bombing and shelling campaign. They told me that it showed that the Vietcong were so demoralised that they were having to take refuge underground. Well I must confess that I bought that version of the story. It was only later when it was discovered how enormous the complex was and how skilfully the Vietcong used them and how the tunnels actually extended under the American base camp itself, that I started to think for myself and I realised that this was not a sign of how demoralised the Vietcong had become but how determined they were.

Booby traps

The Vietcong were especially skilled at planting booby traps (Sources **M** and **O**). Some were simple, such as a concealed hole under a path which could break the ankle of anyone stepping into it. More lethal was the *punji* trap – a deep hole with upturned bamboo or metal spikes with points covered in poison or human excrement (to cause blood poisoning).

Source N
By a war correspondent serving in Vietnam

Source K US soldiers discover the entrance to a Vietcong tunnel

- **Bouncing Betty** was a mine just under the earth's surface. It exploded when a soldier trod on one of the three prongs jutting upwards out of the ground.
- **The tin can trap** was a grenade with the pin removed which was wedged inside a can to stop it from being detonated – until a soldier unwittingly set it off by tripping over a wire.
- **The fuel tank trap** was a grenade with a rubber band around it to stop the firing mechanism detonating the explosives inside. Put inside the fuel tank of an enemy vehicle it was only a matter of time before the rubber perished, detonating the grenade and exploding the fuel in the tank.

Source M Booby traps in Vietnam

According to one historian, 'booby traps accounted for fully 11 per cent of American deaths in Vietnam and 17 per cent of wounds' (Source **N**).

You could be in the most protected space in Vietnam and still know that your safety was provisional, that early death, blindness, loss of legs or arms, major and lasting disfigurement – the whole rotten deal – could come in on the freakyfluky as easily as in the so-called expected ways. The roads were mined, the trails booby-trapped, satchel charges and grenades blew up jeeps and movie theatres.

From *Dispatches* by Michael Herr, Picador, 1978

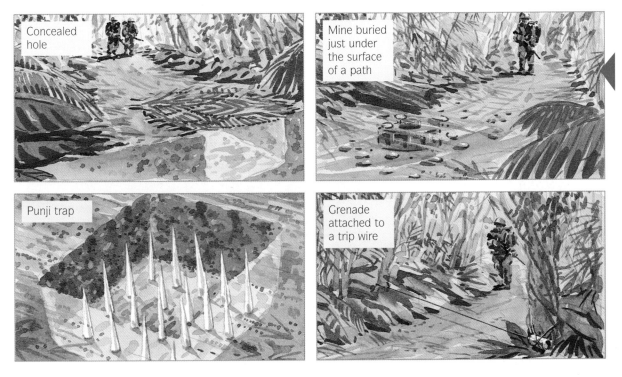

Concealed hole

Mine buried just under the surface of a path

Source O Booby traps used by the Vietcong

Punji trap

Grenade attached to a trip wire

Supplying the Vietcong

The North Vietnamese used the Ho Chi Minh Trail to send guerrillas, weapons, equipment and food to the Vietcong in the South. This 1,000-kilometre routeway wound its way across the forested ridges and valleys of the hills which dominate the borderlands of Vietnam, Laos and Cambodia. Although the name 'Ho Chi Minh Trail' indicates a single routeway, it was much more than that (Source **P**).

Source P By an American officer

Well it wasn't one trail. There were thousands of trails, thousands of rest spots along the way where enemy troops could seek refuge and build up.

From *Vietnam: The Ten Thousand Day War* by Michael Maclear, 1981

In places the Trail was 80 kilometres wide with dummy paths and depots to confuse enemy planes, floating bridges to cross streams, and a workforce of 40,000 people to keep the traffic flowing. Much of it was carefully hidden from the air. The dense tropical forest provided ideal cover with three canopies of trees twenty to thirty metres above the ground obscuring the hive of activity below.

The life and work of the people using the Trail was anything but pleasant. US and ARVN warplanes attacked them when the weather was fine. When it was poor, they were soaked to the skin. The heavy and incessant monsoon rains made the packs carried by the soldiers appear to double in weight, mosquitoes were everywhere and the constant damp gave 'the intolerable impression that mushrooms are about to grow on your clothes and even on your skin'.

Many of the weapons and supplies transported along the Trail came from North Vietnam's allies. The Soviet Union supplied most of the aircraft, heavy guns and surface-to-air missiles. Most of the fuel, ammunition, hand guns and food came from China. A third important supplier was the United States! Huge quantities of American equipment fell into enemy hands and were recycled. Unexploded shells were dismantled and the explosives inside used to make Vietcong booby traps and bombs.

Questions

1 Use the information in the text and the sources here and on pages 26–27 to write a letter home from a US soldier describing the Vietcong, saying who they were and how they fought. Explain the problems that you and your 'buddies' have in combating Vietcong tactics.

2 'The Vietcong's main arsenal [source of weapons] was the United States.' What did the Labour politician Denis Healey mean by this?

3 What part did China and the Soviet Union play in the conflict?

4 Study Source **L**.
a) How and why did Julian Pettifer's later interpretation of the Vietcong tunnels in 1993 differ from the one he was given by the US Army in 1968?
b) What does this tell you about the use of historical evidence?
c) Does this mean that one of these interpretations is necessarily better than the other one?

Search and destroy

▶ *What was meant by search and destroy and how effective was it as a tactic to defeat the Vietcong?*

Hunting the Vietcong

The US Army hunted the Vietcong down rather than let them control the villages and the countryside. Search and destroy was the method they used – sending army units into the field to search for, and kill, any Vietcong they could locate. You can see the methods they used in Sources **A**, **B**, **C**, **E**, **F** and **G**.

Source B   Some search and destroy tactics

Source A   The use of helicopters in search and destroy operations gave the Vietcong very little warning of an attack. Troops could be landed close to the villages and forests they were going to search.

Without uniforms, it is difficult to tell a Vietcong fighter from a loyal South Vietnamese (especially when the 'loyal' Vietnamese is a VC sympathiser). The only way to prove it is to find equipment, food supplies or weapons in the suspect's hut or catch them sneaking out at night with a Kalashnikov [rifle] in his (or her) hand.

Search and destroy missions would go through hamlets with a fine tooth comb. If suspicious gear was found, it was often easier to burn down the whole hut than to drag a hundred pounds of rice back to base and the inevitable paperwork. If weapons were found, however, the Vietnamese would have to face some rigorous questioning.

From *The History of the Vietnam War* by Charles T. Kamps Jr, Hamlyn, 1988

Source C US soldiers on patrol warily following the course of a stream. The surrounding rainforest provided ideal cover for Vietcong waiting in ambush.

The Vietcong followed the same policy as well. They called it 'Find and Kill.' 'Either way, it was us looking for him, looking for us, looking for him', said a soldier. Each platoon or company usually returned to a nearby firebase after a mission but some spent much longer in the field, camping out at night.

Torture and brutality

To frightened soldiers who daily saw their friends blown up on jungle missions, any method, such as the use of chemical weapons (see page 36), was a legitimate way of waging war against a cunning and deadly enemy. US/ARVN search and destroy patrols employed brutality and torture and showed a callous

disregard for human life. But if you read the sources that follow you will understand some of the reasons for their actions even though their deeds are difficult or impossible to excuse.

Source D
Letter home from Thomas Pellaton

You kill because that little SOB is doing his best to kill you and you desperately want to live, to go home, to get drunk or walk down the street on a date again.

Reprinted in *Dear America* edited by Bernard Edelman

When a booby-trapped artillery round blew two popular soldiers into a hedgerow, men put their fists into the faces of the nearest Vietnamese, two frightened women living in the guilty hamlet, and when the troops were through with them, they hacked off chunks of thick black hair. The men were crying, doing this. An officer used his pistol, hammering it against a prisoner's skull.

Scraps of our friends were dropped into plastic body bags. Jet fighters were called in. The hamlet was levelled and napalm was used. I heard screams in the burning black rubble. There were Vietcong in that hamlet. And there were babies and children. But Chip and Tom were on the way to Graves Registration in Chu Lai, and they were dead, and it was hard to be filled with pity.

From *If I Die in a Combat Zone* by Tim O'Brien, 1973

Source F   A member of the 9th Infantry Division passing a burning Vietcong base camp in April 1968

Interrogation

Vietcong suspects were rounded up and interrogated – often brutally – to find out what they knew and to see if they could incriminate others (Sources **G** and **H**).

Source G   US soldiers track down Vietcong enemies

Methodically they searched the house, poking bamboo stakes into walls and into the ground to detect hiding spots and escape tunnels. They soon dragged a number of young men out of a hidden compartment and hustled them off for interrogation. The young lady informant – out of sight – identified those with VC connections.

From *The History of the Vietnam War* by Charles T. Kamps Jr, Hamlyn, 1988

Source H   Interrogating Vietcong suspects

The nightmare of Vietnam

Not surprisingly, many soldiers had nightmares and panic attacks after suffering horrific experiences in the field (Source **I**). Violent images of the war affected many soldiers long after their return to the USA (page 60).

Source I   A US soldier's terrifying memories

I was in the shower when the shaking started. Suddenly thirty hours of terror exploded in my stomach, and I started bawling like a baby. I rushed outside. It all unwound out of me, like a coil spring. Unravelled. Came apart. I saw the explosion on the road again, the crater, the body hanging on the wire. I heard the crushing roar. I smelled the powder and the diesel fuel and the rot and the death.

From *And A Hard Rain Fell* by John Ketwig, 1985

Questions

1   Imagine you are a journalist accompanying a platoon on a search and destroy mission. Use Sources **A** to **I** to write an account for your newspaper describing what happened and what you saw and heard.

2   Design a poster attacking either US forces in South Vietnam, or the NVA, or the Vietcong.

3   Use the sources to write a reasoned account explaining why the search and destroy missions probably did more to advance the Vietcong cause than they did to harm it.

The My Lai massacre, March 1968

▶ **What was the My Lai massacre in 1968 and what were its consequences?**

My Lai village

Soon after dawn on Saturday, 16 March 1968, nine large black helicopter gunships landed close to the small Vietnamese village of My Lai on the coast about 120 kilometres south of the huge American base at Danang. The village consisted mainly of thatch-covered red-brick houses next to a minor road set among hedges, bamboo trees and a paddy field. About 700 inhabitants lived there at the time when the Americans came.

   Three platoons of American soldiers left the helicopters. They were part of a search and destroy mission codenamed Task Force Barker after its overall commander, Lieutenant Colonel Frank Barker. You can see what happened next in Sources **B** to **I**. One of the platoons, led by Lieutenant William Calley, spent the next two hours or so killing in cold blood a large number of unarmed Vietnamese men, women and children.

Source A
Map showing the position of My Lai

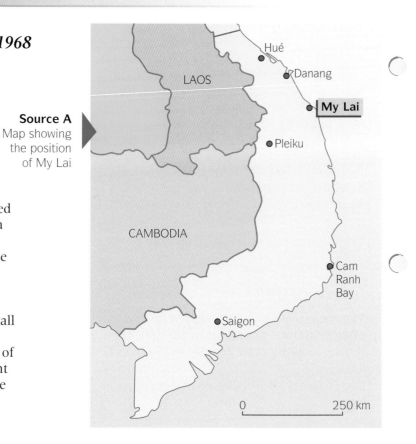

Source B   From a diary written by Thomas Partsch

Got up at 05.30 and we left 07.15. We had nine choppers. We started to move slowly through the village, shooting everything in sight, children, men, women, and animals. Some was sickening. Their legs were shot off and they were still moving. They were just hanging there. I didn't fire a single round yet and didn't kill anybody, not even a chicken. I couldn't.

Quoted in *Four Hours in My Lai* by Michael Bilton and Kevin Sim, Viking Penguin, 1992

We met no resistance and I only saw three captured weapons. We had no casualties. It was just like any other Vietnamese village. As a matter of fact, I don't remember seeing one military-age male in the entire place, dead or alive. The only prisoner I saw was in his fifties.

From *My Lai 4* by Seymour M. Hersh, 1973

Source C   By Sergeant Michael Bernhardt

Source D   By Paul David Meadlo (aged 22)

Source E   By Ronald L. Haeberle, an official army photographer

Lieutenant Calley came over and said, 'You know what to do with them [a group of Vietnamese men, women and children] don't you.' And I said, 'Yes.' And he left and came back about ten minutes later, and said, 'How come you ain't killed them yet?' And I told him that I didn't think he wanted us to kill them, that he just wanted us to guard them. He said, 'No, I want them dead.' So he started shooting them. And he told me to start shooting.

Quoted in *Time* magazine, 5 December 1969

I saw two small children, maybe four or five years old. A guy with an M-16 fired at the first boy, and the older boy fell over to protect the smaller one. Then they fired six more shots.

Quoted in *Time* magazine, 28 November 1969

Why kill?

The villagers were assumed to be Vietcong sympathizers although most of the genuine Vietcong in the village escaped (Sources **F** and **G**).

> Everyone who went into the village had in mind to kill. We had lost a lot of buddies and it was a VC stronghold. We considered them either VC or helping the VC.
>
> Quoted in *Time* magazine, 5 December 1969

Source F By Varnado Simpson (aged 22)

Source G By an American war correspondent

> The few Vietcong who had stayed near the hamlet were safely hidden. Nguyen Ngo, a former deputy commander of a Vietcong guerrilla platoon operating in the My Lai area, ran to his hiding place 300 metres away when the GIs came in shooting, but he could see that 'they shot everything in sight.' His mother and sister hid in ditches and survived because bodies fell on top of them.'
>
> From *My Lai 4* by Seymour M. Hersh, 1973

The evidence

Although the My Lai massacre took place in March 1968, the shocking secrets of this appalling tragedy did not come to light until eighteen months later in November 1969.

On Tuesday, 25 November 1969, Paul Meadlo was interviewed on US television. He told viewers he had killed 'ten or fifteen men, women and children' when his unit entered My Lai. When asked why, he replied: 'I felt I was doing the right thing, because like I said I lost buddies in the fighting.' Most Americans were horrified and public pressure forced the US Army to launch an official investigation (Source **H**). The evidence from the men who had taken part was overwhelming and included photographs taken by an official US Army photographer (Source **I**).

> During the interview T'Souvas admitted the company had murdered four hundred unarmed civilians. He admitted himself shooting a girl aged about 15. He killed four others who were wounded because they wouldn't get medical treatment. 'I wanted to talk about this for a long time and am glad now that it is off my chest. It is wrong. Even before it was investigated I wanted to write about it to my Senator, but I didn't know how to go about it.'
>
> From *Four Hours in My Lai* by Michael Bilton and Kevin Sim, Viking Penguin, 1992

Source H Private Robert T'Souvas interviewed by military police

Source I Murdered women and children after the My Lai massacre. American newspapers were heavily criticised when they reproduced photographs of the massacre. One woman complained: 'How can I explain these pictures to my children?'

Questions

1 What evidence is there that there were Vietcong in My Lai village?

2 Imagine you are an American or Vietnamese eyewitness of the My Lai massacre. Write a letter to a relative in Britain describing what has happened.

3 Use these sources and those on pages 30–31 to explain how the 'search and destroy' operation at My Lai was different and how it was similar to routine operations in other parts of Vietnam.

Obeying orders

As the evidence of the massacre flooded out, some of the soldiers concerned expressed remorse for their actions, some shifted the blame on to others, while a few acknowledged their guilt. Most said they were only obeying orders even though US Army instructions clearly stated that a soldier had a duty to disobey any orders which 'a man of ordinary sense and understanding would know to be illegal'.

Source J Helicopters similar to this Chinook helicopter (seen in action in September 1967) were used in the My Lai operation. It was standard procedure. The US Army had no reason to think My Lai was any different from hundreds of similar missions elsewhere in Vietnam at that time.

There was an order from the Captain. He gave the order. He said there would be no children and there would be no civilians in the village at 07.30. He stated that everything that was there was VC or VC sympathizers. There was no doubt in the men's mind that they [the people in the village] were VC.

We obeyed our orders. If an officer tells me something and I don't do it, I'd find myself court-martialled. He was my superior officer and I had to follow him whether I wanted to or not – personal opinions don't enter into it.

Quoted in *The Times*, 9 December 1969 (adapted)

Source L By Sergeant Hodges

The order we were given was to kill and destroy everything that was in the village. It was to kill the pigs, drop them in the wells; pollute the water supply; kill, cut down the banana trees; burn the village; burn the hootches [houses] as we went through it. It was clearly explained that there were to be no prisoners.

Quoted in *Four Hours in My Lai* by Michael Bilton and Kevin Sim, Viking Penguin, 1992

Justice

Exactly how many Vietnamese civilians were killed was never determined. Official estimates put the number at not less than 175 while it could have been as high as 400 or 500.

Source K By Sergeant Isaiah Cowen

Most of those responsible were never brought to justice and, of those charged with war crimes, all were acquitted except Lieutenant Calley. His attitude was summed up in four words: 'No big deal, Sir.' He later argued: 'We weren't in My Lai to kill human beings, really. We were there to destroy Communism.' Calley was sentenced to life imprisonment with hard labour but came out of prison in 1974 after only three years. As for the other soldiers and officers involved, the authors of *Four Hours in My Lai* summed it up: 'Everyone else responsible for the most inexcusable act of American arms during this century had got clean away with it.'

The Vietnamese at My Lai who survived the massacre, however, will never forget (Source **M**).

I think of it all the time. I think about it and I can't sleep. I won't forgive. I hate them very much. I won't forgive them as long as I live. Think of those children, that small. Those children at their mothers' breasts being killed.

Quoted in *Four Hours in My Lai* by Michael Bilton and Kevin Sim, Viking Penguin, 1992

Source M By Truong Thi Le, who hid in a paddy field while nine members of her family died

Reaction to the massacre in the United States

Most Americans were as horrified as the rest of the world when the massacre made headline news. Many were so appalled they doubted whether it could be true (Source **N**). In some quarters, however, Lieutenant Calley was treated more as a hero than as a killer. A record called *The Battle Hymn of Lt Calley* sold 200,000 copies and was even played on the armed forces radio network in Saigon.

Source O   The Vietnamese civilians murdered at My Lai were little different from these frightened Vietcong suspects photographed in 1966. People at home in the United States seeing a photograph like this found it impossible to credit that ordinary American boys of 19 (the average age of a GI in Vietnam) could find it in their hearts to kill innocent people in cold blood.

Source N   Popular reaction to news of the My Lai massacre

Cleveland woman: It sounds terrible to say we ought to kill kids, but many of our boys being killed over there are just kids, too.

Los Angeles salesman: I don't believe it actually happened. The story was planted by Vietcong sympathizers and people inside this country who are trying to get us out of Vietnam sooner.

Philadelphia office worker: I can't believe our boys' hearts are that rotten.

GI serving in Vietnam: There's gotta be something missing.

Cleveland woman to local newspaper: Your paper is rotten and anti-American.

Another GI serving in Vietnam: The company must have been hit hard before the action.

Former serviceman: No American would ever kill 100 people like that.

Quoted in *My Lai 4* by Seymour M. Hersh, 1973

Questions

1 Using the sources here and on pages 32–33, write a short essay saying what happened at My Lai on Saturday, 16 March 1968.

2 Design a poster accusing US forces in Vietnam of war crimes.

3 Examine each source in turn and list any factors which suggest it may be unreliable and those which suggest it may be useful.

4 Is there any reason to doubt the reliability and accuracy of any of the sources on these pages?

Chemical warfare

▶ *Why were chemicals used by US forces in Vietnam and what effect did they have on humans and on the environment?*

Using chemical weapons

The rainforests gave the Vietcong plenty of cover. US pilots found it difficult to target them from a plane or helicopter. Then the Army came up with the answer: clear the trees and strip away the foliage so there would be nowhere for the Vietcong to hide. They did this in four main ways:

1 Using napalm to burn off leaves and vegetation;
2 Spraying chemical agents (weedkillers) to strip away leaves (a process called defoliation);
3 Dropping huge bombs which could splinter large trees into tiny chips;
4 Making use of giant mechanical ploughs to tear down trees.

In other words, science and technology could defeat the enemy by altering the geography of Vietnam (page 24).

Using napalm

One of the first and worst of these weapons was the use of napalm (jellied petrol). It stuck to its victims, causing horrific burns. You can see what happened in Sources **A**, **B**, **C**, **D** and **E**.

Source C   By an American war correspondent

Source D   By Ho Thanh Dam, a North Vietnamese victim of napalm

▼

Then the bombing began again, this time with napalm, and the village went up in flames. The napalm hit me, and I must have gone crazy. I felt as if I were burning all over, like charcoal, and I lost consciousness. My wounds didn't begin to heal until six months later.

Quoted in *Vietnam: A History* by Stanley Karnow, Viking Penguin, 1991

Source A   Napalm bombs explode in flames in the rainforest

Source B   By Nicholas Tomalin, a British war correspondent

▼

Two F105 jets appear over the horizon in formation, split, then one passes over the smoke, dropping the trail of silver, fish-shaped canisters. After four seconds' silence, light orange fire explodes in patches along an area fifty yards wide by three-quarters of a mile long. Napalm. The trees and bushes burn, pouring dark oily smoke into the sky.

From *The Sunday Times*, 5 June 1966

Sometimes the chopper you were riding in would stop a hill and all the ground in front of you as far as the next hill would be charred and pitted and still smoking, and something between your chest and your stomach would turn over. Frail grey smoke where they'd burned off the rice fields, brilliant white smoke from phosphorus, deep black smoke from napalm. They said that if you stood at the base of a column of napalm smoke it would suck the air right out of your lungs.

From *Dispatches* by Michael Herr, Picador, 1978

Some of the victims from these napalm strikes were so disfigured they 'crept off to live in caves and other remote spots'. Horrific photographs in the Exhibition of American War Crimes in Ho Chi Minh City show the disfigured faces of Vietnamese who had been burned by napalm. One of the most memorable images of the war, taken by a press photographer, was of child victims running away from a burning village (Source **E**).

Source E South Vietnamese children fleeing from a napalm raid

Agent Orange

The Americans also used weedkillers (or 'defoliants') such as Agent Orange, to strip away leaves and undergrowth, leaving the trees and branches bare. Aeroplanes systematically sprayed the forests, almost as if they were using a pesticide on a farm (Source **F**). You can see the effects it had on the countryside in Sources **G** and **H**.

Source F A C-123 Ranch Hand aircraft sprays defoliant over the rainforest in January 1967

Source G The devastation caused by defoliants

I leaned out the door and looked at the endless progression of giant pits which were splashed over the ground, at the acre-sized scars where napalm or chemical spray had eaten away the cover. There was a special Air Force outfit that flew defoliation missions. They were called the Ranch Hands, and their motto was, 'Only we can prevent forests.'

From *Dispatches* by Michael Herr, Picador, 1978

Source H
By an American war correspondent

One Air Force unit whose task was to defoliate the place, also destroyed all the main food crops. The whole country started to look like a leper from the air, a series of gross malformed swimming holes, barren scrags of what once were majestic 300-feet mahogany trees. The very air and water started to take on a total polluted glint, a deathly hue in which the Vietnamese were supposed to enjoy the benefits of a free democratic way of life.

From *Nam* by Tim Page, published in 1983

Unfortunately for the Americans as well as for the Vietnamese, Agent Orange contained a highly toxic chemical called dioxin. It not only poisoned the environment but contaminated the people who handled it at the air base when loading the plane. As a consequence some of the American soldiers concerned contracted cancer.

After it was used, Vietnamese doctors began to report victims suffering from vomiting and headaches. Long-term effects included birth defects and serious skin complaints. By the end of the war, over 25,000 square kilometres of rainforest and cropland had been ruined by defoliants. The mangrove swamps of the Mekong Delta had been almost completely destroyed. But it was not until December 1970 that the US decided to stop using defoliants in Vietnam. This was long after scientists around the world had protested about their use.

Questions

1 Write a US Army press release justifying the use of chemical weapons in Vietnam.

2 Use the sources to explain the effect chemical warfare had on the people and environment of Vietnam.

3 *Either* write a speech *or* draw or paint a poster attacking the American use of chemical weapons in Vietnam.

4 Look at Source **E**. Why did this photograph make such an impact on people throughout the world? In what ways is it different from most of the other photographs in this book?

5 Join a class debate condemning the use of chemical weapons in Vietnam. Speak either for or against the motion.

37

5 Turning point of the war

The Tet Offensive, 1968

▶ **What was the Tet Offensive?**

Vietnam in January 1968

By January 1968, a certain amount of complacency had crept in. Over half a million US soldiers were stationed in South Vietnam. The NVA and the Vietcong had lost nearly 100,000 men in the previous year. General Westmoreland was convinced he was winning the war.

Nguyen Van Thieu had been elected President of South Vietnam in 1967. The US Army had won every set-piece battle, including the hard-fought Battle of Dak To near Pleiku in November 1967 (Source **J** on page 27). US soldiers patrolled the jungles and the hills while the ARVN protected the cities and the coast.

The Tet festival

As the Vietnamese began to observe the Tet festival, celebrating the lunar New Year, US soldiers had reason to think victory could be in sight – until Wednesday, 31 January 1968 (Source **B**).

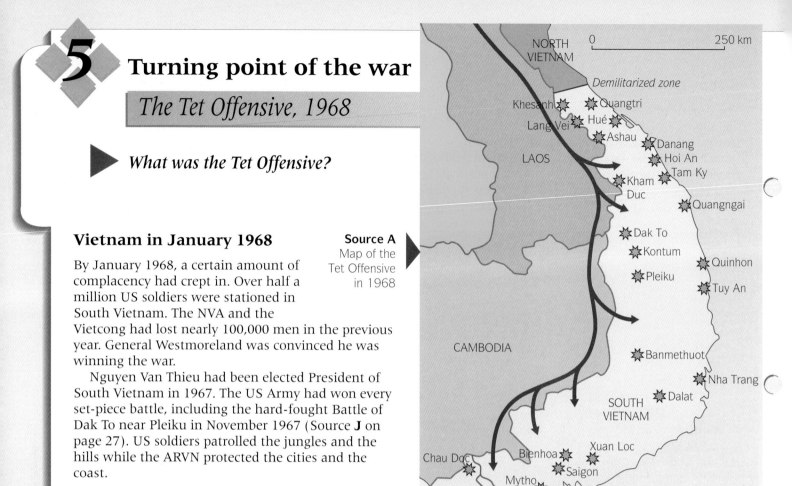

Source A Map of the Tet Offensive in 1968

Key
➤ Ho Chi Minh Trail
✸ Towns and bases attacked by the NVA and Vietcong

Source B Report in *Time* magazine

Suddenly, in a whoosh of rockets and thud of mortars, the nightmare seemed about to begin again. Barely 19 hours after they had ended a self-imposed, week-long Tet truce, Communist gunners launched coordinated rocket and mortar attacks on more than 100 cities, towns and military installations throughout South Vietnam, including the capital of Saigon.

Source C From *The Times*, 31 January 1968

The Vietcong raiders moved under cover of night and the Tet celebrations to infiltrate Nha Trang. Mingling with the gunfire was the crackle of firecrackers tossed by Vietnamese celebrating a few blocks away. Aircraft with loudspeakers pleaded with them to stop so that the troops could tell where the shooting was. They did not seem to hear.

Americans and South Vietnamese alike had assumed the North would be celebrating the Tet festival too. To make matters worse, the sound of enemy rockets and guns became confused with the sound of friendly fireworks celebrating the festival (Source **C**).

Julian Pettifer worked as a war correspondent for the BBC. On 31 January 1968, he began his report with the words: 'The Americans tell us they are winning the war. Well here we are. We're in the centre of Saigon and this gunfire you can hear is pretty close.' At first, the Vietnamese were shocked, especially since their capital city, Saigon, had been attacked (Source **D**).

All at once the war – and the danger – was very real. The fighting was no longer confined to the jungles or the hills. It was countrywide – from the Mekong Delta in the south (Source **E**) to Hué, Khesanh and Danang in the north (Sources **F** and **G**).

Sightseers in Danang, all dressed-up for the Tet holiday, even walked through the city to see where the battle had been fought and to look at the corpses of the Vietcong on open display.

Source D
Report in
The Times,
1 February
1968

Vietcong guerrillas yesterday fought pitched battles with American and South Vietnamese forces in Saigon streets. Snipers in a building near the presidential palace, which was mortared, kept military police and troops at bay despite heavy machine-gun fire from a tank in the street. The fighting followed last night's attack on the American Embassy by a 19-man Vietcong suicide squad, all of whom were killed.

The first night of the Tet Offensive we were in the Special Forces C Camp for the Delta. In the morning there were about a dozen dead Vietnamese across the field there where we'd been firing. Thousands of people died in Vietnam that night, the twelve across the field, a hundred more along the road between the camp and the Can Tho hospital.

From *Dispatches* by Michael Herr, Picador, 1978

Source E   By a war correspondent in the Mekong Delta

The streets of Hué are a wreckage under drizzling rain. Unburied North Vietnamese sprawl in the position in which they died among the dangling wires, twisted trees and buildings half reduced to rubble.

Source F
From *The Times*,
10 February
1968

Khesanh

At one time during the Tet Offensive there were fears that the thousands of soldiers besieged in the US Marine base at Khesanh in the extreme north-west – close to the frontier with North Vietnam – might become the victims of another Dien Bien Phu. The war correspondent Michael Herr, who was in Khesanh, wrote at length about the experience (Source **G**).

Source G   By Michael Herr in Khesanh

We knew that once the monsoons lifted, it would be nothing to drop tens of thousands of tons of high explosives and napalm all around the base, to supply it without strain, to cover and reinforce the Marines. We could all sleep easier for it. All any of us had to worry about was the fact that Khesanh was vastly outnumbered and entirely surrounded; that, and the knowledge that all ground evacuation routes, including the vital Route 9, were completely controlled by the NVA, and that the monsoons had at least six weeks more to run.

From *Dispatches* by Michael Herr, Picador, 1978

Source H   Damage at Saigon during the Tet Offensive in 1968

A calculated risk

The Tet Offensive was a new departure for the Communists since it exposed their soldiers directly to enemy fire. They took a calculated risk. They expected the people of South Vietnam to join them in sweeping away the regime of Nguyen Van Thieu and forcing the Americans to leave the country.

Questions

1   Suggest reasons why Vietcong/NVA forces began their onslaught on the South at the end of January.

2   What does the map (Source **A**) tell you about the Tet Offensive?

3   Write a short account, using the sources on these pages, explaining what was meant by the Tet Offensive.

4   Was Khesanh in danger during the Tet Offensive? Use Sources **A** and **G** to say why it was a prime target for the North Vietnamese.

5   'Yesterday's attacks involved heavy loss of face for President Thieu's government.' Use Source **D** to explain this statement.

How the Tet Offensive decided the war

▶ **What impact did the Tet Offensive have on the war in Vietnam?**

Impact on the North Vietnamese and the Vietcong

All told, over 100,000 people were killed during the Tet Offensive. At first it was seen in the West as a spectacular victory for the North. Yet North Vietnamese leaders themselves considered it a failure (Source **A**).

Source B Impact of Tet on the NVA/VC

▼

Many observers believed it was their last massive effort, and, having been repulsed, their losses were so great that they would never again be able to mount an offensive on such a scale. The lack of civilian support for the NVA/VC during Tet strengthened the South Vietnamese government's claim that the war and the hearts of the people were both being won.

From The Complete Military History of the Vietnam War by Douglas Welsh, Brompton Books, 1990

Source A By North Vietnamese General Tran Do

▼

In all honesty, we didn't achieve our main objective, which was to spur uprisings throughout the South. Still we inflicted heavy casualties on the Americans and their puppets and that was a big gain for us. As for making an impact in the United States, it had not been our intention – but it turned out to be a fortunate result.

Quoted in Vietnam: A History by Stanley Karnow, Viking Penguin, 1991

Significantly, the North Vietnamese agreed to take part, at last, in peace talks soon after the Tet Offensive ended. Until then they had steadfastly refused to sit down at the same table with representatives of the South Vietnamese government.

Source C
Sabotage to an American jeep at Danang in March 1969. Vietcong terrorist attacks continued after 1968 but no longer posed as great a threat to US security as they did before the Tet Offensive.

The Tet Offensive was also a serious setback for the Vietcong – at least 30,000 people were killed – a devastating blow from which they never recovered (Sources **B**, **D** and **E**). Thereafter, the major role in the war was undertaken by the NVA.

Source D
By Sir Robert Thompson, a British expert on guerrilla warfare

The Vietcong had been irretrievably weakened by the Tet Offensive and without Vietcong help the NVA could no longer conduct a guerrilla-type war. Its strategy had to be changed to conventional invasion.

From War in Peace by Sir Robert Thompson, Orbis, 1981

Source E People killed during the Tet Offensive

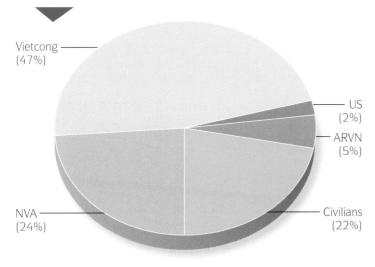

- Vietcong (47%)
- US (2%)
- ARVN (5%)
- Civilians (22%)
- NVA (24%)

Impact on the United States

War coverage in the press and on television had earlier given the American people the impression that victory was almost in sight. When news of the scale and scope of the Tet Offensive sank in, Americans immediately jumped to the conclusion they had been mislead by the Army. Walter Cronkite, the leading American television newscaster, dismayed President Johnson when he read the news agency messages from Vietnam and was heard to say: 'What the hell is going on? I thought we were winning the war.'

In fact, the US Army still thought that. They regarded the Tet Offensive as a victory over the Vietcong/NVA and were dismayed when the media decided it was at best a war that could not be won and at worst a defeat (Sources **F** and **G**). Even worse, these views were shared by the politicians. General Westmoreland was refused when he asked for another 200,000 troops to join the half million GIs already serving in Vietnam.

Nonetheless, the Tet Offensive was the major turning point in the war. It convinced most Americans, rightly or wrongly, that the war had to be ended as soon as possible, otherwise it would go on for years (Source **H**).

Source H Public opinion shifts after the Tet Offensive

Giap had achieved one of his most important goals. He did not win any of the major battles, but the American people had been made painfully aware of the war and its cost in lives. World opinion against the war increased and added to the anxiety of the American people about the legitimacy of their continued role in Vietnam.

From The Complete Military History of the Vietnam War by Douglas Welsh, Brompton Books, 1990

Despite the fact that the North Vietnamese and Viet Cong incurred a military defeat of such proportions that it took them four years to recover, reporting of the Offensive by press and television in the United States gave an impression if not of American and South Vietnamese defeat, then of an endless war that could never be won.

From the foreword to The Vietnam War by Charles B. MacDonald, Salamander Books, 1996

Source F By General William Westmoreland

To American officials, it all added up to a severe defeat for the Communists. But this was not the impression given by the copy and television film footage of American newsmen. To them, the Tet Offensive was an incredible shock, an unmitigated disaster, a clear American and South Vietnamese defeat. Television cameras focusing on one badly damaged block could give the impression of an entire city in ruins. The civilian casualties [some 7,000] and refugees [close to 700,000] generated by the fighting made the headlines – not the 5,000 or more civilians systematically tortured and executed by the Communists in Hué and elsewhere.

From The Vietnam War by Charles B. MacDonald, Salamander Books, 1996

Source G By the Deputy Chief Historian for South-east Asia

The Tet Offensive also forced Lyndon B. Johnson to abandon hopes of seeking re-election as US President. In doing so, he paved the way for the election of Richard Nixon in November 1968 – and Nixon had promised Americans he would end the war. The pressure to begin peace talks (pages 48–55) became unstoppable.

Questions

1 Look at the pie diagram (Source **E**). Who suffered most during the Tet Offensive? Explain the reasons for this.

2 Using the evidence in the sources say whether you agree with the US Army view that the Tet Offensive was 'a severe defeat for the Communists'?

3 To what extent are the results of the Tet Offensive described in Source **A** supported by the other sources on these pages?

4 What effect did media coverage of the Tet Offensive have on public opinion in America? Why was it a major turning point in the war?

6 The peace movement in America

Protest and the media

▶ **How did the experience of war lead to the growth of the peace movement in America? What was the role of the media in the growth of the peace movement?**

The draft

US involvement in Vietnam first made an impact on the American people when the government was forced to draft (conscript) many more young men into the armed forces than in previous years. Only 3,000 men a month had been needed in February 1965. When eleven times as many – 33,000 a month – were called up in October, opposition to the draft rapidly mounted. Those who avoided the call-up were called 'draft-dodgers' (Source **B**).

Source A Swearing young men into the US Army

> Everybody's fighting to stay out. They bring their parents, their bosses, their lawyers. They run out and get married to somebody they shouldn't. They go back to college. They bring in phoney certificates from doctors. Everybody's got an angle.
>
> Quoted by Gerald Priestland in *From Our Own Correspondent: The First Forty Years* edited by Tony Grant, Pan, 1995

Source B By a draft board chairman

Many men burned or tore up their draft papers (Source **C**). Some fled to Canada or Europe. Muhammad Ali, the world heavyweight boxing champion, even had his title taken away from him after resisting the draft.

There was widespread resentment, however, that many educated, affluent and middle-class Americans could find legitimate ways of avoiding or postponing the draft, leaving the poorer Americans, many of them black, to do most of the fighting (Source **D**).

Source D By surgical nurse Pat Johnson, who served in Vietnam

> I remember having really angry feelings about the people who had gotten out of being there, because a lot of these kids in Vietnam were really young and they were so far away from their families.
>
> From *A Piece of My Heart* by Keith Walker, 1985

Source C US draftees setting fire to their call-up papers

The killing field

As the fighting intensified, hundreds of American soldiers were killed in action, most of them in their teens. It reached a peak in May 1968 when 562 soldiers were killed in a single week (Source **D** on page 59). The fact that 5,550 Vietcong also died was no consolation for grieving relatives in the USA. The real horror of the war began to sink home. It hit small communities especially hard, as Micki Voisard, a woman airline attendant flying into Vietnam, recalled after reading about a former schoolfriend who had been killed (Source **E**).

Then it hit me that he was dead. He was the hometown all-American boy. Every girl in my high school was in love with him. He was the special one. He was president of the student body and quarterback on the football team. The whole town gave him a send-off party to Vietnam. They sent him off to war. And when he was killed, it was amazing what happened. His father committed suicide. His mother had to go in a home. People just couldn't accept this. They mourned for weeks.

From *A Piece of My Heart* by Keith Walker, 1985

Hey! Hey! LBJ! How many kids did you kill today?
Bring our black GIs home
Oppose this war
Draft beer, not boys
Dump Johnson
Eighteen today, dead tomorrow
War Criminal Westmoreland
No fighting for racist USA
Get us out of Vietnam now
Give peace a chance
Hell no, we won't go
Who are we to police the world?

Source F Anti-war slogans

Protest!

The ultimate sacrifice paid by these soldiers seemed pointless and led to riots and demonstrations. Students in many American colleges and universities demonstrated on campus (pages 46–47). Some of the slogans they used can be seen in Source **F**.

Support for the war

To many Americans, however, the war was simply a question of right against wrong. So although the anti-war protests made the biggest headlines, there were demonstrations in favour of the war too (Sources **H** and **I**).

Source G
President Lyndon B. Johnson (LBJ) was said to have been 'heart-broken' when he heard the chant: 'Hey! Hey! LBJ! How many kids did you kill today?'

America, love it or leave it
I wish I had a draft card [slogan carried by a girl]
Bomb Hanoi
We love America
Love our country
Your flag, your future
My country – right or wrong
Will we let them bury US?
No glory like old glory

Quoted in *The Glory and the Dream* by William Manchester, Michael Joseph, 1974

Source H
Pro-war slogans

New York. 27 March 1966. More than 50,000 anti-Vietnam demonstrators paraded down Fifth Avenue all afternoon yesterday, pelted by eggs and an occasional fist, to cheer speakers at a Central Park rally. Thousands of spectators lined the route to heckle the marchers as 'Communists' and 'cowards' and to show their support for the Johnson administration's policy in Vietnam.

From the *International Herald Tribune*, 28 March 1966

Source I Report of an anti-Vietnam protest

At the start of 1968, a Gallup Poll showed that 46 per cent of the American people still approved the President's handling of the war and 50 per cent believed it essential the Communists be prevented from taking over South Vietnam.

Questions

1 What was meant by the draft? Why did it make such an impact on American society?

2 Explain the cartoon (Source **G**).

3 Design a simple banner which a peace protester could have carried in a demonstration in the late 1960s.

4 Use the sources to explain the reasons for the growth of the peace movement in America.

The veterans' protest

As the casualties mounted, however, the demonstrations got bigger and bigger. Over 100,000 protesters demonstrated outside the Pentagon in Washington in 1967. Four years later, a huge crowd of 300,000, took part in the Veterans' March (Source **K**). This was one of the most moving and significant demonstrations against the war because the protesters had actually fought in the war themselves. These were not 'draft-dodgers'. Many were heroes. Some were on crutches and wore their old uniforms. When they threw away the decorations, medals, ribbons and honours they had been given for fighting in the war, many Americans were deeply shocked.

Rusty Sachs, a helicopter pilot, who had gone out as an excited young volunteer in 1966 feeling that 'there was something noble about it', came back disillusioned and threw his hard-won medals away as well. 'It was pain,' he said. 'It was real pain, because we were rejecting things that had been so important to us.'

Source K The Veterans' March, Washington DC, 25 April 1971

William Wyman, from New York City, is nineteen, and has no legs. He sits in a wheelchair on the steps of the United States Congress, in the midst of a crowd of 300,000, the greatest demonstration America has ever seen. He has on green combat fatigues and the jacket is torn where he has ripped away the medals and the ribbon he has been given in exchange for his legs. Along with hundreds of other veterans of the war in Vietnam, he has hurled them on the Capitol steps.

From *The Last Day* by John Pilger, Syndication International, 1975

Make love not war

Many Americans said the war was immoral. The US government had no right to impose its views on a poor nation like Vietnam. Leading scientists criticised the use of chemical weapons and the effects they were having on the environment.

The protests were strongest among young people. This was the late sixties and early seventies: a period noted for mini-skirts, punk rock, exotic hairstyles, civil rights, race riots, drug abuse, and mammoth outdoor rock festivals, such as Woodstock in 1969. Many teenagers 'dropped-out' of society in protest. The 'hippies' told people to make love not war. It is 'the only meaningful response to Vietnam', they said.

Source J
Disabled veteran of the Vietnam war at the Vietnam War Memorial in Washington DC

The role of the media

The media played an important part in exciting protest. The war in Vietnam was the first to be covered night after night on television. It made people viewing at home realise what was being done to Vietnam in their name. Photographs in magazines and newspapers had a similar impact. Film and photographs of the Buddhist monk who set himself alight helped to convince President Kennedy that Vietnamese President Diem should be replaced (page 15).

Source L A demonstration in Washington against the Vietnam war

Two images in particular affected the way people thought about – and later remembered – the war (Source **N**). One was a photograph showing screaming Vietnamese children after a napalm attack (Source **E** on page 37). The other showed the cold-blooded execution of a Vietcong officer in the street (Source **M**).

Source N   A former UK student leader, David Triesman, interviewed in the 1990s

There was more than anything else a sense of the injustice of it and a sense of horror, perhaps at seeing the first war where day by day you saw the most appalling atrocities come back through your evening news. Small children on fire, people being shot – prisoners just being shot in front of you. It would have been a pretty insensitive population of young people in this country which didn't react to it.

From *People's Century: 1968 – New Release*, a BBC TV programme transmitted on 20 January 1997

Source M   Street execution of a Vietcong suspect by the Saigon police chief in 1968

One-sided coverage of the war

US Army commanders and many officers and soldiers were dismayed at the media coverage of the war, and even blamed television and the press for weakening the American stance in Vietnam (Source **F** on page 41). It was the media, however, not the US Army, which first exposed the scandal of the My Lai massacre eighteen months after it took place in 1968 (pages 32–35).

Nonetheless, the generals had a point. There was little media coverage of the war from the Communist side. Reporters could not go out on patrol with NVA or Vietcong units to describe their failures and report on their war crimes. It was much easier to follow the Americans.

North Vietnamese atrocities, such as cutting off the heads and genitalia of US soldiers killed in action, were rarely shown since the very limited coverage provided by the North Vietnamese authorities was carefully organised and monitored. As a result, the newsreel sequences screened in North Vietnam were very one-sided. They showed the world what Ho Chi Minh wanted them to see: 'a peasant nation bravely resisting the might of America'.

Questions

1 Which photographs do you think David Triesman remembered when he talked about Vietnam some 25 years later on television (Source **N**)?

2 Study Sources **F** and **H** on page 43. Write three additional slogans for each of the following:
a) The Veterans' March in 1971;
b) Government supporters after the Tet Offensive in 1968 (pages 38–41).

3 Trace or copy the photograph in Source **M** and use arrows and labels to point out details which explain why world reaction to this picture was so strong.

4 Draw or paint a government poster aimed at getting the support of young Americans for US policy in Vietnam.

5 Use Source **N** and Sources **F** and **G** on page 41 to describe and discuss the impact that the media had on the public during the Vietnam war.

Kent State University, May 1970

▶ **What happened at Kent State University in 1970 and what was its effect on the peace movement in America?**

The campus protests

Most of the protests and demonstrations against the war in Vietnam were peaceful but noisy. They became more violent in 1970 after US troops invaded Cambodia (page 50). Anti-war protesters in California set fire to a bank in February and threw rocks and bottles at police. There were protest marches and demonstrations at colleges and universities across America. Long rows of students taunted the police (Source **A**).

In some states, part-time soldiers – called National Guardsmen – were brought in to help the police keep order. Most were inexperienced and easily panicked. This led to a fatal confrontation at Jackson State University in Mississippi where two students were shot dead by police.

Source A US marshals bodily remove American protesters at a demonstration

Confrontation

The worst incident occurred at Kent State University in Ohio in 1970. On Saturday, 2 May, over 800 students demonstrated on the campus and one of the university buildings was burned to the ground. By Sunday night all was quiet. But the next day – Monday, 4 May 1970 – the demonstrations took a sinister turn (Sources **B** to **F**).

Source B From the *International Herald Tribune*, 6 May 1970

On the grassy commons behind the administration building, several hundred students massed to continue their protests against the war and against the presence of the guardsmen. Hundreds of other students were on nearby slopes surrounding the commons. Other students were leaving their classrooms, walking to lunch through the area. Guardsmen carrying loaded rifles with bayonets fixed, were lined up facing the students on the green. They stood with their backs to the charred shell of the building destroyed on Saturday night.

Officers in two Jeeps rolled across the grass to address the students with bullhorns: 'Evacuate the Commons area. You have no right to assemble.' Back came shouts of 'Pigs off campus! We don't want your war.' Students raised middle fingers. The Jeeps pulled back. Two skirmish lines of Guardsmen, wearing helmets and gas masks, stepped away from the staging area and began firing tear-gas canisters at the crowd.

Then the outnumbered and partially encircled contingent of Guardsmen ran out of tear gas. Suddenly they seemed frightened. They began retreating up the hill, most of them walking backward to keep their eyes on the threatening students below. When they reached the top, some Guardsmen knelt quickly and aimed at the students hurling rocks from below. A handful of demonstrators kept moving toward the troops. Within seconds, a sickening staccato of rifle fire signaled the transformation of a once-placid campus into the site of an American tragedy.

Source C From *Time* magazine, 18 May 1970

Source D Ohio National Guardsmen fire tear gas at students at Kent State in 1970

'They are shooting blanks – they are shooting blanks,' thought Kent State Journalism Professor Charles Brill, who nevertheless crouched behind a pillar. 'Then I heard a chipping sound and a ping, and I thought, 'My God, this is for real.' The shooting stopped – as if on signal. The campus was suddenly still. Horrified students flung themselves to the ground, ran for cover behind buildings and parked cars, or just stood stunned. Then screams broke out. 'My God, they're killing us!' one girl cried. They were. A river of blood ran from the head of one boy, saturating his school books. One youth held a cloth against the abdomen of another, futilely trying to check the bleeding.

Source E From *Time* magazine, 18 May 1970

Source F A student screams after a friend had been killed at Kent State

Consequences

Four students were dead, none of them remotely fitting the description applied to them by the Governor of Ohio who had called the demonstrators Communists, likened them to Hitler's Brownshirts, and said that they were 'the worst type of people that we harbour in America'. Ten other students had been wounded. A tearful friend of one of the students asked: 'Have we come to such a state in this country that a young girl has to be shot because she disagrees deeply with the actions of her government?'

The massacre sparked off hundreds of protests across America. The student strike centre at Brandeis University claimed that lecturers and students in over 450 colleges and universities had gone on strike (Source **G**). Over 70 people were injured in a New York demonstration.

With peaceful strikes and violent marches; with flower-draped crosses, black arm bands and anti-war buttons; with firebombs, window smashing and stone throwing – American college students showed their sorrow and their rage at the widening of the war and the fatal shooting of four students in Ohio.

The callous disregard for human life, and the stifling of the right to protest in a democratic society, caused widespread revulsion throughout America and the rest of the world. It put extra pressure on the US government to find a peaceful way of ending the conflict.

Source G By Robert Siner in the *International Herald Tribune*, 6 May 1970

Questions

1 Imagine yourself as one of the following:
   a) a student protester,
   b) a bystander,
   c) a member of the National Guard,
   d) a university lecturer.
   You are standing on the commons at Kent State University on 4 May 1970. Write a letter to a friend in England describing in detail what happened and the effect it had on you.

2 What reasons help to explain why so much fuss was made over the deaths of four students at Kent State at a time when over 57,000 other young Americans were dying in Vietnam?

7 Ending the war: 1969–75

Peace talks

▶ *Why did peace talks begin in 1968?*

First steps to peace

The search for a peaceful solution to the conflict began as early as 1966 but did not become urgent until after the Tet Offensive in 1968 (pages 38–41). Each time the US government tried to involve the United Nations in getting peace talks started (in January 1966 and again in September 1967), the North Vietnamese refused to cooperate. They insisted that US forces must leave Vietnam first.

Towards the end of 1967, however, the North Vietnamese let it be known that they might be prepared to talk if the USA halted its bombing campaign in the North. Responding to this on 17 January 1968, President Johnson said he would do so if talks could be arranged promptly and with a reasonable chance of success. But he insisted that neither the Vietcong nor the North Vietnamese should take advantage of any lull in the bombing. He got his answer a fortnight later when the Tet Offensive began (pages 38–41). As a consequence, the Americans felt betrayed – as if the Vietcong had stabbed them in the back.

As you have seen (page 41), however, the North Vietnamese suffered severe losses during the Tet campaign. When President Johnson broadcast his intention of withdrawing from the 1968 presidential election and suspending the bombing campaign in the North, he was surprised by the response he got from Hanoi (Source **A**).

The news media's negative handling of the Tet Offensive caused the President to yield to increased pressure from anti-war critics, and from civilian officials in his government, and proclaim another bombing halt – with yet another invitation to the North Vietnamese to negotiate. To add weight to his initiative, Johnson also announced that he would not be a candidate for the presidency in the Autumn of 1968. To his surprise, the Vietnamese agreed to talk.

From *The Vietnam War* by Charles B. MacDonald, Salamander Books, 1996

Source A   By the Deputy Chief Historian for South-east Asia

Disadvantages of being a democracy

The North Vietnamese government had one big advantage over the American government. It did not have to account for its actions to an electorate or to a parliament. It was under no pressure to make concessions. Instead, it was tightly controlled by a small committee called the politburo which was chosen by the ruling Communist Party. This consisted of Ho Chi Minh (until his death in 1969); General Giap as Defence Minister; Le Duc Tho, Chief Negotiator at the Paris peace talks (Source **C**); Pham Van Dong, the Prime Minister; Le Duan, First Secretary of the Communist Party; and two other leading Communists.

Source B   Delegates to the Vietnam peace talks meet round the conference table in Paris

The Paris peace talks

The peace talks in Paris begun by these moves dragged on for five years. At times there was complete stalemate. Both sides raised many objections. South Vietnam objected to the Vietcong being present at the talks. The Communists responded to American proposals with 'our rejection is firm, total and categorical'. The Americans greeted Communist proposals with 'old wine in new bottles'.

America, by contrast, underwent a change of leaders. In January 1969, Lyndon Johnson, a Democrat, was replaced as President by Richard Nixon, a Republican. Nixon and his Chief Foreign Adviser and negotiator, Dr Henry Kissinger (Source **C**) both wanted to bring the war in Vietnam to an end as soon as possible. During five years of negotiations, public hostility to the war continued to grow. This put extra pressure on Nixon to fulfil his election promise to bring the war to an end.

Source C Le Duc Tho (right) and Dr Henry Kissinger (left) in Paris. In the centre is Tho's interpreter.

Peace aims

The United States and its allies wanted South Vietnam to be left alone to determine its own future without 'foreign' (meaning Hanoi, China and the Soviet Union) interference. Reunification with North Vietnam would only be possible if *all* Vietnamese voted in favour at free elections.

North Vietnam demanded the following conditions:
1 The complete withdrawal of US troops;
2 A return to the Geneva Agreement of 1954;
3 South Vietnam to be left to manage her own affairs;
4 Peaceful reunification without 'foreign' (meaning the United States) interference.

As you can see, both sought freedom from foreign interference and both meant something different by 'foreign'.

Détente

The actions and intentions of Nixon and Kissinger have also to be seen in the context of the Cold War. Relations between East and West had been improving during the 1960s, despite the American commitment to Vietnam. *Détente* had already led to important agreements, such as the Test Ban Treaty in 1963. Neither side wished to jeopardise this relationship.

At the same time, American diplomats had also improved US relations with Communist China (Hanoi's other main ally besides the Soviet Union). Relations between China and the Soviet Union, however, had worsened and had even led to shots being fired across their common frontier (Source **D**). Nixon made skilful use of this split between the two Communist giants by visiting China in February 1972 and the Soviet Union three months later in May (page 53). Lack of unity in the Communist camp made it easier to negotiate a cease-fire.

We have been sincere and unsparing in our efforts to assist Vietnam. The hostility toward us of the pro-Chinese elements in Vietnam has been a bitter pill to swallow. Without material aid from the Soviet Union, it would have been impossible for Vietnam to survive under the conditions of modern warfare and to resist as rich and powerful an aggressor as the United States.

From *Khruschev Remembers* translated by Strobe Talbot, Little, Brown, 1970

Source D By Nikita Khruschev, ex-leader of the Soviet Union

*Q*uestions

1 List the reasons which help to explain why both sides agreed to hold peace talks in 1968.

2 Why did the peace talks fail to bring results at first?

3 How did democracy prove a hindrance to the United States at the peace talks?

4 What effect did *détente* have on the peace talks?

Vietnamization

▶ *What was meant by 'Vietnamization' and what effect did it have on the course of the war?*

Expanding the ARVN

In June 1969, President Nixon announced the withdrawal of 25,000 US troops from Vietnam. In future, South Vietnam would take over its own defence with the aid of US weapons, arms and equipment. US troops would withdraw as and when ARVN forces could take their place. The new policy was called 'Vietnamization' (Source **B**).

Source A The first US Marines prepare to leave Vietnam in July 1969

Source B Vietnamization

The basic principle was that South Vietnam would slowly take over all civil and all military aspects of the war. Vietnamization meant that the South Vietnamese government had to put its own house in order if it wanted to survive.

From *The Complete Military History of the Vietnam War* by Douglas Welsh, Brompton Books, 1990

Source C
South Vietnamese soldiers on patrol in the Mekong Delta

Even at this late stage in the war, South Vietnam had not yet brought in full-scale conscription – even though hundreds of thousands of American boys had been drafted into Vietnam to fight on their behalf. In the next few years, as the ARVN expanded to over a million men, US armed forces left Vietnam in stages, handing over their arms and equipment to the South Vietnamese troops who had been trained to take their place.

Vietnamization went so well that in April 1970 Nixon announced plans to withdraw 150,000 troops. He told Americans: 'This far-reaching decision was made after consultation with our commanders in the field and it has the approval of the government of South Vietnam.' But as James Reston commented in *The Times*: 'The distinction is clear. He "consulted" his commanders in the field but did not get their "approval".'

In fact, US Army commanders were furious. They still believed they could win the war. But Nixon himself was in a no-win situation. Demonstrations against the war were becoming more vocal and more violent (pages 46–47) and his opponents thought he wasn't moving towards peace fast enough.

Cambodia

Despite this, Nixon was still prepared to take military action against the NVA even if it meant escalating the war. One month after the pro-American government of Lon Nol seized power in neighbouring Cambodia in March 1970, Nixon caused a violent storm of protest (pages 46–47) when he ordered a 'friendly' invasion with the 'limited' objective of driving the NVA out of their sanctuaries in Cambodia.

Democracy in South Vietnam

By the end of 1971, the US Army had withdrawn 400,000 troops leaving behind only 140,000 soldiers. Nixon promised that most of the rest would go in 1972. By this time, however, it was clear that the US had failed to turn South Vietnam into a Western democracy. President Thieu ruled more as a dictator than as a democrat. He imprisoned political opponents and, when a presidential election was held in 1971, tried to buy votes to secure victory. His chief opponent refused to stand against him, saying he could not 'put up with a disgusting farce that strips away all the people's hope of a democratic regime'.

US troops lose their enthusiasm

While most people in the United States welcomed the slow withdrawal of US troops, the process had a disastrous effect on Army morale in Vietnam. No one wanted to be the last to die in battle for a lost cause. Search and destroy missions became 'search and avoid' operations. Over-enthusiastic officers were threatened and even murdered (Sources **E** and **F**).

Source D Once withdrawal of troops became official policy, most soldiers had only one aim: to leave Vietnam alive

From 1969 a grim new word was used by the army in Vietnam – 'fragging'. In plain English, murder. It derived from the use of a fragmentation weapon, usually a hand-grenade, as the surest way of getting rid of an unpopular officer. Between 1969 and 1971, according to official data, the total number of 'fragging incidents' was 730 and eighty-three officers were killed this way. But these figures do not include assaults on officers with other weapons – rifles or knives.

From *Vietnam: The Ten Thousand Day War* by Michael Maclear, 1981

Source E 'Fragging' incidents

The number of deserters and soldiers absent without leave rose sharply. Racism also become a problem since America's blacks sensed they had been given a larger share of 'the Vietnam experience' than their actual numbers in the USA warranted, although this was denied by the Army.

Many soldiers took refuge in alcohol and drug abuse (Source **F**). Ever since the start of the war, this had been one way of coping with the horrific nature of the war, the loss of close friends, and the prospect of imminent death.

Source F US troops become indifferent

The year 1971 saw a series of stories revealing the massive heroin problem among United States troops [about one in ten was addicted], the 'fragging' of unpopular officers [forty-five killed, 318 wounded in 1971], the staggering desertion rate, the number of combat refusals, and the growing tendency to regard an order simply as a basis for discussion. GIs were photographed carrying peace symbols, a picture appeared in *Newsweek* of a helicopter with a sign on the side saying 'My God! How'd we get into this mess?' and CBS News ran film of GIs smoking pot from a gun barrel.

From *The First Casualty* by Phillip Knightley, André Deutsch, 1975

1 Explain briefly what was meant by:
   a) Vietnamization,
   b) Fragging,
   c) Combat refusal,
   d) Peace symbol.

2 Use Sources **E** and **F** to make a list of the things which tell us the US troops had lost their enthusiasm for the war.

3 Write a reasoned account explaining how and why the phased withdrawal of US troops from Vietnam helped to demoralise the US Army.

4 How did Vietnamization affect the course of the war?

Forcing North Vietnam to submit

▶ **What effect did the US bombing campaign have on North Vietnam in 1970–72? How important were Le Duc Tho, Nixon and Kissinger in bringing peace to Vietnam?**

A first test for Vietnamization

For four years, from mid-1968 to April 1972, the ground war was quiet as US troops left Vietnam and were replaced by the newly 'Vietnamized' forces of South Vietnam. Enemy activity had been muted after the collapse of the Tet Offensive. According to General Westmoreland (Source **F** on page 41), it took the Vietcong and NVA four years to recover.

But war erupted once more in 1972 when the NVA, armed with tanks and artillery, invaded the South on a scale far greater than in 1968. Hanoi expected an easy victory since most of the US troops had gone. On 30 March 1972, they launched a massive campaign, led by 100 Soviet tanks. Vietnamization was about to be tested in full (Sources **A** and **B**).

Linebacker

President Nixon, no longer able to mount a counter-attack with US ground forces, responded in the only way he could. In April he ordered the air force to bomb the North. A huge armada of carrier-based warplanes joined forces with B-52s flying out of Guam and Thailand. Many of the earlier restrictions were removed. The bombing offensive, codenamed Linebacker, destroyed North Vietnamese roads, lorries, trucks, tanks, railway lines and storage depots. The port of Haiphong was devastated. Smart bombs – guided by lasers – pinpointed enemy targets. Bridges which had escaped earlier raids were destroyed.

The resumption of bombing was not simply a military response to the North Vietnamese invasion. It had a political purpose as well. Nixon and Kissinger were trying to 'persuade' the North Vietnamese negotiators to give way in Paris. A government official said they were forcing the North Vietnamese to decide 'whether the offensive is worth continuing and whether they have the means to continue it'. By bombing fuel dumps and supply lines, the USA hoped to bring the invasion to a halt by cutting off supplies of fuel for Giap's tanks.

Not until the eve of Easter Sunday, four days after the beginning of the massive artillery barrage, was it clear that a major assault was under way. By then, some 10,000 North Vietnamese regulars were driving straight through the Demilitarized Zone into Quang Tri province to join another 20,000 troops already in the area. Taking advantage of heavy rains and low clouds, which limited air strikes, other units rolled down French-built Highway 1 aboard Soviet-built tanks and trucks towing anti-aircraft or artillery pieces.

1 May 1972:
Thousands of South Vietnamese soldiers of the Third Infantry Division, most of whom did not appear to have seen much combat with the advancing North Vietnamese troops, today fled in a confused stream south down Highway 1 from Quang Tri province. They commandeered civilian vehicles at rifle point, carried away rations but not ammunition, and threw stones at Western news photographers taking pictures of them. No one tried to control the troops. Their officers were fleeing too.

Demonstrations and protests

The renewed bombing campaign was greeted with a storm of protest across the world. Student protest campaigns began again in the USA with renewed passion. Demonstrations were held at a number of universities and lecturers and students in over a hundred colleges went on strike for a day. Over 50,000 protesters marched through New York and 210 demonstrators were arrested in Palo Alto in California.

Sidestepping the superpowers

Nixon and Kissinger always knew there was a risk that China, or the Soviet Union, or both, would intervene. But, as you have seen (page 49), Nixon had already taken steps to undermine Hanoi's reliance on her giant Communist allies by arranging summit meetings with both the Russians and the Chinese.

Nixon gambled that Soviet President Brezhnev would want to reach an agreement with the USA more than he would want to back Hanoi. He was right. The summit meeting took place in Moscow a month after the bombing offensive resumed. A beaming Brezhnev greeted a smiling Nixon. A similar reception had earlier greeted Nixon when he visited China earlier in the year in February 1972 (Source **C**).

Source C President Nixon on the Great Wall of China during his visit in 1972

Christmas 1972

Three months after the resumption of bombing, there was a breakthrough at the peace talks in Paris. The North Vietnamese indicated that they were prepared to do a deal. Hanoi's chief negotiator, Le Duc Tho, proposed a cease-fire and Dr Kissinger accepted this as the basis for a peace settlement.

But when the talks stalled once more, Nixon stepped up the pressure and launched the biggest bombing campaign yet at Christmas 1972. A hostile US Senator called it 'the most murderous aerial bombardment in the history of the world.' Mines were laid in the sea close to the harbour entrance to Haiphong, drastically reducing the ability of the port to deal with incoming ships bringing weapons and ammunition from China and the USSR. Round-the-clock B-52 bombers dropped bombs on all the main centres of population supported by F-111s, F-4 Phantoms, and other carrier-based warplanes off the coast of North Vietnam. Over 36,000 tonnes of bombs were dropped on Vietnam in a matter of days, causing enormous destruction to the North.

Source D Scene of devastation after another heavy air raid on Hanoi

Questions

1 How effective were US tactics in Vietnam between 1969 and the end of 1972?

2 How and when did the United States try to force the North Vietnamese to agree peace terms in Vietnam and with what success?

3 Use Sources **A** and **B** to say whether the evidence shows that Vietnamization was:
   a) a success, or,
   b) a failure.

The cease-fire agreement

The Christmas 1972 bombing campaign had the desired effect. The peace talks in Paris were renewed in January 1973 and led at last to an agreement (Source **E**) negotiated by Nixon's Secretary of State, Dr Henry Kissinger, and the North Vietnamese spokesman, Le Duc Tho. President Nixon assured the American people that his government had got 'the right kind of peace – a peace that would last'. Later that year, Dr Kissinger and Le Duc Tho were jointly awarded the Nobel Peace Prize for their work in negotiating the cease-fire. However, Western reactions to the cease-fire were mixed (Sources **F**, **G** and **H**).

Source F   By British expert, Sir Robert Thompson

In reaching a cease-fire agreement in January 1973, Le Duc Tho proved more than a match for Henry Kissinger. The Americans were out and, as for the agreement, the members of the politburo knew that at the right moment they could drive tanks through it.

From *War in Peace* by Sir Robert Thompson, Orbis, 1981

In fact, only trouble could come from permitting North Vietnam to hang on to the areas of the South which it controlled at the time of the cease-fire. What is more, the agreement was unsupervised. There was little anyone would be able do to stop North – or South – Vietnam from breaking the terms of the agreement (Source **G**). To make matters worse for the South Vietnamese, the Americans treated the cease-fire as if it was the end of the war. In reality, it gave the North time to recover. The NVA was strengthened in preparation for a final assault.

Source E   The Paris Peace Agreement, 27 January 1973

- Cease-fire to take effect from 28 January 1973.
- US armed forces to withdraw completely.
- NVA to remain in areas of South Vietnam they control at the time of the cease-fire.
- All foreign forces to leave Cambodia and Laos.
- Elections aimed at reuniting Vietnam to be held.
- All US prisoners of war [mainly aircrew] to be returned by North Vietnam.
- US mines off North Vietnam to be cleared by US minesweepers.
- North Vietnam to recognise the South Vietnamese government.
- An International Commission for Control and Supervision – Hungary, Poland, Canada and Indonesia – to monitor the cease-fire.

Source G   By General William Westmoreland

The cease-fire agreement was theoretically workable – if the threat (and reality) of American airpower remained. By adopting the Amendment [later passed by Congress] which prohibited 'any funds whatsoever to finance directly or indirectly combat activities by the United States military forces in, over, or from off the shore of North Vietnam, South Vietnam or Cambodia', the United States Senate took away that threat.

From the foreword to *The Vietnam War*, Salamander Books, 1996

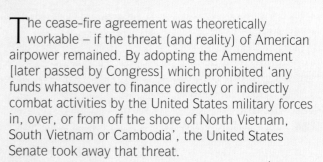

The New York Times:

If it does not guarantee peace, this historic pact at least provides the framework and opportunity for a new era of compromise and conciliation in Vietnam and elsewhere. For the United States, the agreement signals the end of a nightmare. It promises the speedy and safe return of American troops and prisoners and an opportunity for fresh beginnings on neglected problems at home and abroad.

The Baltimore Sun:

A few initials, or for that matter a few signatures, cannot settle in any permanent way the problems of Indo-China. The war will go on.

The New York Daily News:

One sure fact emerges amidst the confusion and the uncertainties. The United States has laid down its policeman's club, at least for this generation. The people simply will not stand for it. Never again can American armed forces be committed to combat without the full and whole-hearted support of the American people.

Source H
US newspaper comments on the cease-fire, 24 January 1973

Reactions in South Vietnam

In South Vietnam, where it really mattered, the government refused to sign the document (Source **I**) and the reception it received in the country was muted.

Source I   By South Vietnamese President, Nguyen Van Thieu

Let me say frankly of the peace accord that I consider it only as a cease-fire agreement. As to whether or not we will have real peace, we must wait and see.

Quoted in *The New York Times*, 24 January 1973

Soon afterwards, the country began to disintegrate. US aid to South Vietnam was drastically reduced, partly because many Americans thought it was no longer necessary since a cease-fire had been signed. Unfortunately for South Vietnam, the US Congress and American media had another enemy to pursue: President Richard Nixon himself. His involvement in the Watergate scandal dominated the news and forced Nixon to leave office. Distrust of the President also prompted Congress to take away his freedom to wage war in Vietnam – with disastrous consequences for the South.

US prisoners of war

The United States stuck to its part of the bargain and US Navy minesweepers had cleared away the mines in North Vietnamese waters by mid-1973. The North Vietnamese responded by returning about 600 prisoners of war by the end of March. In fact, 2,500 US airmen had been shot down and Americans refused to believe that all had died. For many years after the war, rumours persisted to the effect that some American POWs were still alive in North Vietnam.

Source J   Dr Kissinger signing the 1973 cease-fire agreement

Source K   Former prisoner of war, Captain Robert L. Strim, is greeted by his family on returning from imprisonment in North Vietnam

uestions

1 How did the US newspapers (Source **H**) differ in their reaction to the cease-fire?

2 What effect did the bombing campaign have on the outcome of the peace talks?

3 Describe the different ways in which people reacted to the cease-fire.

4 Which sources show there was opposition to the agreement?

5 Describe the achievements of Dr Henry Kissinger and Le Duc Tho. Why were they given the Nobel Peace Prize?

6 'The people of South Vietnam have been guaranteed the right to determine their own future without outside interference.' Was this true?

The fall of Saigon

 ### What reasons help to explain the fall of Saigon in 1975?

A country falling apart

After the cease-fire, almost all US forces withdrew from South Vietnam leaving behind a tiny band of advisers. Meanwhile, rising inflation and a growing unemployment problem brought fresh unrest to South Vietnam. The cease-fire broke down as both sides tried to improve their military positions. In 1974 North Vietnam made big gains when the ARVN abandoned bases in outlying towns.

The South Vietnamese government had assumed that American economic aid would continue but Nixon, entangled in the Watergate scandal, was unable to help. The US Congress refused to prop up the South Vietnamese economy any longer, particularly since corruption was widespread. The country began to fall apart.

Renewal of the war

When North Vietnam renewed the offensive in 1975, making further significant gains, panic set in and South Vietnamese opposition rapidly collapsed (Sources **A**, **B** and **C**).

Source B

A news report in *The New York Times*, 19 March 1975

Source C Thousands of refugees flee from the advancing Communist armies in 1975

Source A By Brian Barron in a BBC broadcast

Hong Kong, January 1975: The South Vietnamese army, the ARVN, is in a worse mess than ten years ago, when the US came to the rescue just as the Communists were threatening to do what they have now done with arrogant ease: cut the country in half. Many people outside Vietnam believe the government soldiers are at worst a cowardly rabble and at best no match for the North Vietnamese. Hours before Danang fell, I watched drunken, barefoot soldiers reeling past groups of military policemen who took no notice. About the same time, at Danang airbase, an army colonel pulled out a fragmentation grenade and tried to hijack a plane to the South. He was shot.

From *Our Own Correspondent: The First Forty Years* edited by Tony Grant, Pan, 1995

A vast exodus of refugees from South Vietnam's Central Highlands is underway, with rear-guard troops blowing up military installations and civilian stragglers burning down their houses. According to one estimate, farmers, businessmen, mountain tribes and soldiers were strung out for 140 miles along the only open road to the safety of the sea coast last night.

The final thrust

New US President, Gerald Ford, tried to help but Congress turned down his request to send additional military aid. Within weeks, South Vietnam folded and the ARVN resistance collapsed.

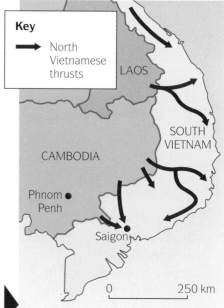

Key
→ North Vietnamese thrusts

LAOS

SOUTH VIETNAM

CAMBODIA

Phnom Penh

Saigon

0   250 km

Source D

Map to show the North Vietnamese advance in 1975

As you can see from the map (Source **D**), NVA troops from bases in Cambodia and Laos launched attacks, using tanks to cut South Vietnam in three and isolate ARVN units in between. Then they turned southwards towards Saigon and marched in at the end of April – less than a fortnight after the nearby Cambodian capital of Phnom Penh fell to the Communist Khmer Rouge at war with the US-backed Cambodian government of Lon Nol (page 50).

Source E
Communist tanks enter Saigon in April 1975

Chaos in Saigon

As you can see from Sources **F** to **H**, there was chaos in Saigon when the North Vietnamese tanks entered the city (Source **E**). There was also chaos at sea when helicopters full of panic-stricken Americans and Vietnamese landed on top of one another on US aircraft carriers offshore. Machines were thrown overboard to enable others to land.

Source F From the *International Herald Tribune*, 30 April 1975

South Vietnamese fled their homeland today in hundreds of small boats, in planes of the Saigon regime's air force and, in one case, in a charter aircraft that a jeep had prevented from taking off until 15 South Vietnamese, led by a colonel, had clambered aboard the plane. An estimated 50,000 persons were on small craft in the South China Sea, heading towards South Korean, Japanese and Taiwanese vessels that were about 10 miles off.

Dodging bullets from bitter South Vietnamese troops and fighting off desperate civilians, Americans fled Saigon today in a 13-hour airlift by an armada of 81 helicopters guarded by 800 Marines and US fighter planes overhead. The helicopters landed at Tan Son Nhut Airport and on rooftops at the US Embassy compound to pick up most of the remaining Americans and many Vietnamese. America's 30-year involvement in the Indochina war was ended in tumultuous scenes, with US Marines and civilians using pistol and rifle butts to smash the fingers of Vietnamese clawing at the 10-foot wall of the US Embassy. Some tried to jump the wall and landed on the barbed wire. A man and woman lay on the wire bleeding. People held up their children, asking Americans to take them over the fence.

Source G
From the *International Herald Tribune*, 30 April 1975

Source H
Panic and fighting as Saigon falls in April 1975

Source I Reactions in America

General Westmoreland:
We failed.

Future US President Ronald Reagan:
We let an ally down.

Leading Democrat Hubert Humphrey:
What we've learned is that there aren't American answers for every problem in the world.

Quoted in *Chronicle of America*, Longman Chronicle, 1989

Questions

1 Why was peace difficult to maintain in Vietnam between 1973–75?

2 Use the map (Source **D**) and Sources **A** to **H** to explain how and why South Vietnam disintegrated so rapidly in 1975.

3 Four events helped North Vietnam become victorious:
   a) The Tet Offensive in 1968,
   b) The withdrawal of American troops in 1969–73,
   c) The failure of the US to support South Vietnam in 1973–75,
   d) Stronger leadership in the North than in the South.
   Which do you think were the most important? Give your reasons.

8 After the war

Failure in Vietnam

What reasons help to explain why the Americans failed in Vietnam?
What were the short-term and long-term effects of the American defeat?

Why the United States lost

After the war, a British journalist wrote: 'One question Americans have been asking themselves is why the greatest military power in history failed to defeat a small Asian army dressed in pyjamas.' Some of the underlying reasons – apart from crucial events such as the Tet Offensive – are listed below.

1 **Soldiers:** Most of the US troops were unwilling and inexperienced conscripts, unused to a life of hardship or to the tropical jungle and its hot, damp climate. They were fighting thousands of kilometres from their homes on foreign territory against enemy soldiers fighting for their homeland. They didn't have the same incentive to fight as the NVA and Vietcong.

2 **People:** The Vietcong made an effort to win over the people in the countryside. The brutal behaviour of ARVN and US troops hunting the Vietcong had the opposite effect, turning many peasants into Vietcong recruits or sympathisers.

3 **Inadequate leadership:** US military leaders had been trained to fight conventional wars with tanks and guns. They never found a really effective way to combat the terrorist methods and guerrilla warfare practised by the Vietcong. Many ARVN leaders were corrupt, incompetent and often cowardly. Under good leaders the South Vietnamese soldiers fought bravely and with skill.

4 **Airpower:** The Americans relied too much on air power despite the lessons of history, such as the failure of the London Blitz to break the spirit of Londoners in 1940–41. 'Once again the fallacy of expecting a determined nation to succumb to bombing from the air has only made the North more resolute and stubborn in their long fight', wrote the historian Edgar O'Ballance in 1970.

Source B
Victims of the air war included the American pilots who were shot down over North Vietnam. Their humiliation was publicised worldwide when the Vietnamese used a picture of captured US pilots guarded by women militia on their postage stamps.

6 The body count: Measuring the success of the search and destroy missions by the total numbers of Vietcong killed converted the conflict into a computerised war of numbers, displaying a callous contempt for the enemy and diminishing the men who fought and died on both sides. It turned many bystanders as well as soldiers against the war (Source **C**).

Y ou come home, and they give the body count each night at dinnertime. They say, 'North Vietnam lost fifteen hundred and we lost thirty. Isn't that great!' You know, to me that's where we really lost it, on that body count. Nobody thought of thirty individuals. Those guys got lost in there, somehow. Fifty-eight thousand people got lost in that body count.

From A Piece of My Heart by Keith Walker, 1985

Source C By flight attendant Micki Voisard, who worked with US soldiers in Vietnam

5 Public opinion: The American media – newspapers, magazines, radio, television – turned against the war after the Tet Offensive (pages 38–41), the My Lai massacre (pages 32–35) and the Kent State massacre (pages 46–47). Photographs, newsreel film, press reports and comment changed public opinion about the war. Stanley Karnow, in *Vietnam: A History*, wrote: 'The real pressure on the Nixon Administration to reach a settlement in Vietnam came from the American public, which by that time wanted peace at almost any price.'

7 The Domino Theory: Insistence on the Domino Theory (page 13), and the long-standing (if misguided) belief in a worldwide Communist conspiracy against the West, stopped America's leaders from seeing the Communist world for what it really was – split into factions dividing China from the Soviet Union, China from North Vietnam, and Vietnam from Cambodia and Laos (Source **E**).

8 Inappropriate technology: US commanders put too much faith in ultra-modern technology. Helicopters, missiles, lasers, and radar could not protect foot soldiers from the dangers of the *punji* trap, land mine or ambush.

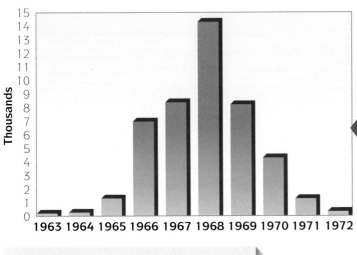

Source D US soldiers killed in Vietnam

Questions

The historic enmity [hatred] between China and the Vietnamese ensured that the only Communist power which had good relations with the Vietcong, or with the Communist government in Hanoi, was the Soviet Union, not China.

From The Time of My Life by Denis Healey, Michael Joseph, 1989

Source E
By Labour statesman Denis Healey

1 Which of the underlying reasons **1** to **8** do you think are most helpful in trying to understand why the Americans failed in Vietnam?

2 Make a list of the crucial events, such as the Tet Offensive, which helped to bring about a defeat for American policy in Vietnam.

3 'The Americans were not defeated in battle yet they lost the war.' Why was this? Write a short account explaining why the Americans failed in Vietnam.

4 How effectively did the USA contain the spread of Communism in Vietnam?

Effects of the war on the United States

'The impact of the war is likely to influence American life for many years to come', wrote James Reston after the signing of the cease-fire agreement in January 1973. Some of these effects were short-term, hitting hard at the time (such as the Kent State massacre). Other effects were long-term and lasted for years after the war ended in 1975. Some even affect the United States today, such as the reluctance of many Americans to see their country intervene in the internal affairs of another country, such as in Bosnia in the early 1990s.

1 **Cost:** The huge cost of the war – £100,000,000,000 – caused taxes to rise and led to inflation. Since so much money was needed to pay for the war, US forces elsewhere were left short of men, money and equipment.

2 **Medical effects:** Soldiers who had handled chemical weapons, such as the highly poisonous Agent Orange, were more likely than other servicemen to contract cancer and have children born with deformities. As many as half a million veterans suffered serious mental problems. Many had recurrent nightmares, recalling the horrors they had seen or inflicted on the enemy. A war correspondent said that after returning to New York, he woke up one night and knew that his 'living room was full of dead Marines' (Source **F**).

> I know a guy who had been a combat medic [army doctor] in the Central Highlands, and two years later he was still sleeping with all the lights on. We were walking across 57th Street one afternoon and passed a blind man carrying a sign that read, MY DAYS ARE DARKER THAN YOUR NIGHTS. 'Don't bet on it, man', the ex-medic said.
>
> From *Dispatches*, by Michael Herr, Picador, 1978

Source F
A war correspondent in New York

Source H
Washington's Vietnam Memorial Statue

3 **Social effects:** Instead of being treated as returning heroes, the 2,600,000 Vietnam veterans were unjustly treated as second-class citizens. They were seen as being losers, no matter how bravely they had fought. Some firms even discriminated against veterans, making the assumption that all were as bad as the worst. Some soldiers reacted to this by taking to a life of violent crime. Many veterans took years to adjust to civilian life. Compared with other Americans, returning soldiers were more likely to turn to crime, alcohol, drug addiction, suicide, or suffer broken marriages. In particular, Vietnam was blamed for the massive drugs problem in the USA in the 1970s and 1980s (page 51).

4 **Disrespect for authority:** Critics blamed the Vietnam crisis for a decline in respect for authority. One parent said: 'We were brought up to never question authority. The government was right and the policeman was right and the priest was right and Mam and Dad were right. Anybody in authority knew what was best and how we should think and they told us how to think.' This view was supported by James Reston writing in 1973 (Source **G**).

Source G
From *The New York Times*, 24 January 1973

> There has been a sharp decline in respect for authority as a result of the war – a decline in respect not only for the civil authority of government but also for the moral authority of the schools, the universities, the press, the church and even the family.

5 **Defeat for a Superpower:** Many people across the world were delighted to view the American failure in Vietnam as a humiliating defeat for the most powerful nation on Earth at the hands of one of the poorest and smallest countries. It was an enormous blow to American pride in their country. Many Americans turned against the idea of Uncle Sam (United States) as the world's policeman. 'No more Vietnams – we've got enough problems of our own' were attitudes which affected US policy for many years.

6 **Racism:** Vietnam was even blamed for increasing racial tension in the United States since many blacks, rightly or wrongly, believed their young men had done a disproportionate amount of the fighting.

7 **War crimes:** US forces in Vietnam were accused of committing war crimes:
   • Dropping 4 million tonnes of bombs on Vietnam;
   • Killing or disfiguring people with napalm;
   • Using chemical weapons, such as Agent Orange and other poisons.

8 Culture: A large number of novels, poems, movies, television shows, plays, paintings and sculptures about Vietnam were produced after the war:

• *Music:* Pop songs stressed the theme of peace, such as the songs of Bob Dylan and John Lennon. The war even inspired the musical *Miss Saigon*.

• *Art:* Painters and sculptors expressed their feelings about the war in their pictures and sculptures (Source **H**). An abstract painter changed his style in 1970 in despair at US involvement in a war which many thought unnecessary, immoral and cruel.

• *Cinema:* Only one major film about Vietnam, *The Green Berets* starring John Wayne, was made while the war was being fought. But from the late 1970s onwards, films about the conflict streamed out of Hollywood, such as *Apocalypse Now*, *Good Morning Vietnam*

(a disc jockey's view of the war), *The Deer Hunter*, *Full Metal Jacket*, *Platoon*, *Born on the 4th of July* (a disabled veteran looks back), *Rambo: First Blood, Part II*, and over seventy other movies.

Source I Scenes from a) *Platoon*, b) *Apocalypse Now* and, c) poster for *The Deer Hunter*

Questions

1 How well does the memorial sculpture in Washington (Source **H**) sum up the role played by ordinary soldiers in Vietnam?

2 What does the bar chart (Source **D** on page 59) tell you about the course of the war in Vietnam? Explain the peaks and troughs in the chart.

3 Make a list of the short-term and long-term consequences of the war. What did the United States gain? What did it lose?

4 How effective was Eisenhower's Domino Theory (page 13) as a forecast of what would happen in Vietnam if US forces withdrew?

5 What are the advantages and disadvantages of using movie films as historical sources?

Impact of the war on Vietnam

▶ *What effect did the war have on Vietnam and the Vietnamese people?*

Source A Huge bomb craters in North Vietnamese paddy fields

Source B By North Vietnamese Prime Minister, Pham Van Dong

> Yes, we defeated the United States. But now we are plagued by problems. We do not have enough to eat. We are a poor, underdeveloped nation. Waging a war is simple, but running a country is very difficult.
>
> Quoted in *Vietnam: A History* by Stanley Karnow, Viking Penguin, 1991

Source C South Vietnamese orphan playing near an M-16 rifle

Aftermath of defeat

The war created a massive refugee problem (Source **C** on page 56) as hundreds of thousands of South Vietnamese fled from the advancing North Vietnamese soldiers early in 1975. The repressive measures which followed increased the misery in the defeated South. The North Vietnamese took charge. Saigon was renamed Ho Chi Minh City and former supporters of the South Vietnamese government were taken away and 're-educated'.

Widespread unemployment and starvation became pressing problems for the people. Corruption in high places and a black market in essential goods made matters worse. Some of these problems were acknowledged and addressed by the North Vietnamese government (Source **B**).

Effect on the people

The war left Vietnam in far worse shape than it did the United States. Nearly four million Vietnamese had been killed or wounded. The South lost 250,000 soldiers dead and 600,000 wounded while the North and the Vietcong lost 900,000 dead and 2 million wounded. As a consequence, there were hundreds of thousands of orphans, maimed civilians and wounded soldiers to care for after the war (Source **C**).

Effect on the environment

Air raids, shellfire, the use of napalm, and chemical agents had scarred the countryside. They left behind a badly damaged environment littered with crashed or damaged warplanes, vehicles and guns, and a landscape pitted with unexploded bombs, shells, booby traps, bullets and land mines. An adventure playground in Hanoi built after the war even made use of relics from the fighting, with children using shot-down fighter aircraft as climbing frames and playing with rusting guns (Source **C**).

A fifth of Vietnam's forests had been destroyed as well as much of its farmland. Twenty years after the war farmers were catching fish and cultivating wildlife in the massive crater lakes left behind as a result of the B-52 bombing raids (Source **A**).

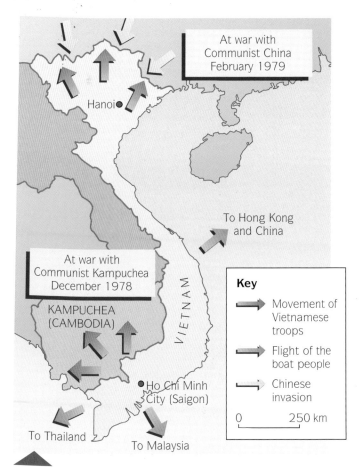

Source D Map of Vietnam after 1975

Map labels:
At war with Communist China February 1979
Hanoi
At war with Communist Kampuchea December 1978
KAMPUCHEA (CAMBODIA)
VIETNAM
To Hong Kong and China
Ho Chi Minh City (Saigon)
To Thailand
To Malaysia

Key
Movement of Vietnamese troops
Flight of the boat people
Chinese invasion
0   250 km

The frail fishing boat, packed with some 250 men, women and children fleeing Vietnam, arrived off the east coast of Malaysia early last week. When it tried to dock at Pulau Bidong, an island that holds Malaysia's largest camp of Vietnamese refugees, police prevented the landing. The craft headed for the mainland, but villagers waded into the water and pushed the vessel away from the shore. In desperation, the refugees attempted to negotiate turbulent waters into the mouth of the Trengganu River. Catastrophe struck. The boat hit a sand bar and capsized. A few dozen aboard managed to swim ashore. More than 200 lost their lives.

Effect on the economy

The aftermath of the war also had serious economic effects since it caused the collapse of the once-thriving Vietnamese economy. These economic problems were made worse when the United States imposed trade barriers making it difficult for the Vietnamese to buy and sell goods to other countries.

Peasants who had joined the Vietcong became disillusioned when their land was taken away. Private farms were taken over by the state and turned into collectives like those in China and Russia. This affected food production already ruined in some areas when napalm and chemicals were sprayed by the Americans to strip away vegetation. Rice production and the growing of fruit crops were both badly hit.

The boat people

In 1978–79, the 'confrontation between the feuding Communist armies of Indo-China' (when North Vietnam went to war with her neighbours, Cambodia and China) uprooted about a million refugees. Already suffering from starvation and the repressive policies of the regime, they decided to emigrate – illegally and by boat. The plight of these desperate people, most of them of Chinese origin and discriminated against by the Vietnamese, caught the imagination of the world. It was called the flight of the boat people (Source **E**).

Source E
Boat people crowded on to a boat after leaving Vietnam

An estimated 50,000 drowned or were attacked and murdered by pirates. News reports claimed that one boat had been attacked seven times by pirates who even took away their food and water. The problem was made worse when many countries, such as Malaysia (Source **F**), tried to turn them away. The refugees fought with police and tried desperately to land. Some boats were deliberately sunk to stop the authorities towing them out to sea. The lucky ones survived and nearly a million were accepted as refugees in the West, most of them in the United States.

Source F From *Time* magazine, 4 December 1978

Questions

1 Make a list of the different ways in which the war affected Vietnam and the Vietnamese people in the years after the war. Which were the short-term and which were the long-term effects?

2 Who were the boat people and why was their fate a world problem in the late 1970s?

Index